CHILD
PSYCHOTHERAPY

CHILD PSYCHOTHERAPY

From Initial Therapeutic Contact to Termination

SOPHIE L. LOVINGER, PH.D.

JASON ARONSON INC.
Northvale, New Jersey
London

This book was set in 12 pt. Bembo by Alpha Graphics of Pittsfield, New Hampshire, and printed and bound by Book-mart Press, Inc. of North Bergen, New Jersey.

Library of Congress Cataloging-in-Publication Data

Lovinger, Sophie L.
    Child psychotherapy : from initial therapeutic contact to termination / Sophie L. Lovinger.
      p. cm.
    Includes bibliographical references and index.
    ISBN 0-7657-0084-0 (alk. paper)
    1. Psychodynamic psychotherapy for children.   2. Developmental
therapy for children. I. Title.
RJ505.P92L68   1997
618.92'8914—DC21   97-10296

Printed in the United States of America on acid-free paper. For information and catalog write to Jason Aronson Inc., 230 Livingston Street, Northvale, New Jersey 07647-1731. Or visit our website: http://www.aronson.com

Contents

9
Dreams   151

*Research on the dreams of children from a developmental
perspective within the context of traditional theorizing about
dreams, and how to deal with the dreams of children.*

10
Termination   163

*The issues and problems of termination of treatment with
children, and assessments of when treatment is at an end.*

Acknowledgments

I give my heartfelt thanks to the many people who have assisted and supported me in the development of this book. First among them is my husband, Bob, who patiently read draft after draft helping me to clarify my thinking and sharpen the presentation. Sandra Lynn Benaway read the first, dreadful draft and did not discourage me. Brenda Lovegrove-Lepisto provided some semblance of organization. Dr. Michael Moskowitz was willing to look at yet another book on child therapy, and production editor Elaine Lindenblatt provided further organization and tightening of the manuscript.

Virginia Axline, my first supervisor, demonstrated responding to a child in a down-to-earth fashion. It had a powerful impact on my development as a child therapist. There were many others along the way, too numerous to name, who have contributed to my development. However, the most profound force on my growth, development, and understanding has come from the hundreds of children I have worked with over the years of my professional life. Many of them have thrived and gone on to lead productive and satisfying lives. Some of them have not been able to make it, while others I have failed. No matter the outcome, they have all had an impact on me and I have been enriched by knowing them, walking that painful path to full and adequate functioning with them, and being there with their joys and sorrows. To all, thank you.

Introduction

Treating the child with dignity and respect is the major emphasis of this book. Closely allied with this emphasis is engaging the parents in the therapeutic process. The parents, as my at-home co-therapists, begin to establish a quasi-therapeutic milieu that serves to help them develop empathic communications/connections with their child and enhances the therapy.

Family therapy seems to be the current treatment of choice when children present problems, as the difficulties are considered to arise from perplexing family interactions. While family problems do have a deleterious impact on a child's functioning, what gets lost in family treatment is the impact of difficult family interactions on the child. The problems of family functioning become a part of the individual's style of functioning. While family treatment can help all family members deal with their interpersonal functioning, it does not have an impact on intrapersonal organization. However, dealing with internal, intrapsychic organization can make for enduring changes in the child.

Child therapy has a very different beginning from adult therapy. It is not the child who makes contact with the therapist, saying, "I have a problem I would like to talk to you about." Rather, it is the parents who contact the therapist, saying, "My child has a problem." Children, especially during middle childhood—the years from approximately 6 to 12, function as if nothing were wrong or bothering them, in hopes that the problem will go away. Children fear that talking about problems will make the problems worse. Thus, it is the parents who typically initiate therapeutic contacts because of their, or teachers', physicians', or other professionals', concerns about the child's functioning.

Seeking help is a difficult step for most individuals, but especially for parents. They experience this decision as a confession of their inadequacy; they have not been able to raise a child without problems. The parents may initiate the contact in the hopes that their concerns are not as serious as they fear, that the problem lies within the child and not with them or their child-rearing practices, and/or that the issues can be dealt with simply and rapidly. Parents, particularly mothers, initiate therapy for their children with much ambivalence and a generalized expectation that the professionals are going to blame them for all the difficulties their children experience. This maternal expectation fairly accurately expresses the state of our field.

Caplan and Hall-McCorquodale (1985), in reviewing the literature describing the origins of psychopathology, found that the patterns in every category they examined resulted in mothers being blamed. They concluded that mother-blaming is a common practice in clinical journals, while the roles of father, other relatives, schools, or other relationships and institutions are not considered as possible contributors toward the problems in living encountered by children. They write, "The present study had demonstrated that mother-blaming is a significant and serious problem that continues in the current clinical literature. For mothers' sakes, clinicians' tendency to blame mothers must be curbed" (p. 352).

Professionals encourage parents to feel guilty about being the prime cause of a child's difficulties. Laying a heavy burden of responsibility on the parents, especially the mother, has served to undermine the confidence of people to be adequate parents. The plethora of "how to" books on child rearing seems to confirm the sense of insecurity many people feel regarding child-rearing practices.

In comparison to the incidence of adequate parenting, the incidence of abuse, neglect, and maltreatment of children is low.

Thus, most parents are "good enough parents." Nevertheless, all parents fail, for no one adult can possibly satisfy all the needs of a child, nor is it necessarily desirable, because moderate frustration is important for growth.

Mothers have always had the prime responsibility for child rearing even when intact families were more common than they are now. Fathers have usually been peripheral figures in the process. However, the quality of the father's support is critical, making him an important partner in child rearing. So firmly is the theory of the mother's sole role in the development of children entrenched in psychology, that until the last ten or so years, there had been little research on the father's role in child development.

Research (Lynn 1974, Parke 1981) suggests that when fathers concur in child-rearing practices, especially those that are faulty, emotional difficulties arise. When fathers present an alternative model of child-rearing practices, the child is much less likely to have emotional problems.

Parenting involves both a mother and father and begins before a child is born. When a child is conceived, it automatically becomes a part of an ongoing relationship. How the issues of impending parenthood are handled depends on current life situations, past history, and personal resources. The old conflicts of childhood flare and need to be re-resolved, which inevitably requires the reorganization of one's relationship with one's parents. In addition alterations in one's own self concept must be made to allow for this major life shift of parenthood.

The course of parenthood is also influenced by the characteristics of the baby, first by its appearance and then gradually by its responses. However, the first month after birth, parents and child are primarily engaged in adaptations, attachment, and bonding to one another. The bonding process involves the development of parental attachment to the infant eventuating in the development of what Winnicott (1958) called the "holding environment." Attachment is the child's emotional connection with the parents that enables good psychological development to occur. These processes are two-way streets, as parents and child interact with and influence one another. Hence, the infant too has a role in the development of the parent–child relationship. The culmination of this early history of the parent–child relationship, along with the whole course of development, is brought with the family to the first contact with a therapist.

In my intake procedures (Chapter 1), I make a point of telling parents that the description of the problems they are experiencing with the child is from their perspective, and that to gain as full a picture as possible I need to understand how the child views the problems she is experiencing and to learn the child's conceptions of difficult issues for her. Therefore, I always have a psychological assessment of the child done, sharing the findings with both parents and child. It is from the intake and psychological data that I make my recommendations.

Chapter 3 discusses the type of room I use for child therapy. Knowing that children have a very hard time talking directly about issues of prime importance to them, I have a well-stocked playroom where the child can comfortably move around and play out those issues of critical importance to her. It is not enough to just have a room with appropriate toys to use to convey thinking, feeling, and questioning. It is also important to understand those communications and from what levels of development they may be arising. Chapter 3 also presents the emotional and cognitive development of the child as succinctly as possible, linking play themes with the issues children deal with as they mature.

The chapters that follow discuss treatment issues that are encountered in all therapies: beginning treatment, intervention/interpretation, transference-countertransference, resistance, dreams, and termination. Throughout I have used vignettes from actual therapies to clarify theoretical and practical issues in the treatment of children.

This book presents treatment from a dynamic point of view, looking at issues that children might not readily express, but that often interfere with adequate, developmentally appropriate functioning. Reading a book is not a substitute for good training and supervision. However, it can establish standards for what treatment can be.

1

INITIAL
THERAPEUTIC
CONTACT

Beginning with the first telephone call, therapists assess the strengths, weaknesses, and problems inherent in a family that are leading to strained relationships and to a child in difficulty.

> When Mrs. A. called for a psychological evaluation of her 9-year-old daughter, Wendy, she was quite matter-of-fact. She mentioned that her child had been in a class for the educable mentally impaired for the past three years and that since she had made no progress, the school personnel were going to place her in the trainable classroom. Mrs. A. said she did not want this to occur. She had had Wendy evaluated by the pediatrician who had done a complete physical with genetic, endocrinological, and neurological workups, all of which came back negative. The doctor recommended a psychological evaluation, and that was why she was contacting me.
>
> Mrs. A. seemed to be a well-controlled woman who would do whatever an authority figure told her was needed in the best interest of her child. However, feelings of distress and anger were patently missing. Her manner on the phone also suggested the possibility of aloofness and distance in her relationship with her child.

Mrs. A. readily accepted an appointment time, complying with my wish to see both her and her husband but not Wendy at this first interview. Nevertheless, she arrived alone, stating that her husband was working. During the course of the interview, we discussed Wendy and her two older siblings and the mother's feelings and concerns for this child. It was not until the evaluation process had been completed that I became aware that Mrs. A. did not discuss the father. I did not meet him, nor did Wendy talk about him. He was as silent and unobtrusive as this child who was found to have a severe language disability. Both father and Wendy were the ignored people in this verbal family.

With the telephone contact we look at how the adults present the problems that are distressing to the family, and at how they respond to the probes and inquiries we make. The therapist is also forming her own reactions, and begins to assess the parents' probable commitment to the therapeutic process, as well as other issues that might have impact on the therapeutic process. However, before we can consider these strengths and weaknesses within the family, we do have to meet the family. Whom do we see?

All members of the family should be seen as all are involved in the difficulties of each of the members residing in the same home. Thus, we can experience, first hand, the interactions in a family, and gain impressions of each member. My personal preference is to see both parents without the child for the initial intake interview. This approach provides the parents with the privacy they need to talk about issues of concern to them. I have found that when children are present, the parents are more likely to circumvent some issues while exhibiting discomfort with others. One of my emphases in doing child therapy is to help parents reestablish the lost empathic bonds with their children (Ornstein 1976). Seeing the parents without the child helps me to develop an important relationship with the parents, laying the foundation for the parents to be my co-therapists at home with their child. In this manner they feel they are an important part of the therapeutic process, which can speed the course of treatment and lessen the possibility of children being removed from treatment before the important work has been completed.

When parents bring the child with them I still try to see the parents alone, if that is feasible. With a school-age child, I request that the child remain in the waiting room while I talk with the parents and then invite the child into the consultation room for a brief discussion with the family as a whole and to let the child know what is going to happen.

> Mr. and Mrs. B. asked me to evaluate their 8-year-old son, Greg, who they thought was seriously depressed about the custodial arrangement of staying with his father and stepmother one week and his mother the following. I asked to see the father and stepmother alone, but when they arrived at my office, Greg was with them. I asked Greg to remain in the waiting room while I talked with his parents. During the intake both father and stepmother were quite active in responding to my queries, with the father often deferring to his wife regarding the psychological state of his son. At the end of the intake I invited Greg to join us. He immediately sat on his father's lap with his back to his stepmother. Father began questioning him about the issues both adults had been discussing with me, to allow me to hear the child's own responses. Greg was quite reluctant, as one would expect, and kept his face hidden in his father's shoulder. The stepmother, quite obviously, took a back seat to the discussion. Both parents agreed that the behavior Greg was exhibiting was typical for him; he was usually unresponsive.

My experience with this family led me to conclude that they were concerned about Greg's functioning, and wanted to help him become more lively and vivacious, but were out of tune with the child. They were both aware that the child felt on the spot during this intake, and probably in other situations as well, and how his unresponsiveness was related to it. But they did not seem able to help the child understand what they had been saying about him and their concern over his apparent unhappiness. Therapy with the child alone did not seem to be the best way to remediate the problems this family was presenting. Rather, treatment for the child with collateral treatment of the marital couple and the natural mother seemed crucial for Greg's well-being.

A preschooler cannot be left alone in the waiting room as parents are being interviewed. Therefore, when parents arrive with such a young child I ask them all to join me in the consultation room.

> I received a call from a mother who stated that she was having trouble with her 3½-year-old daughter "minding." She came just with her youngster to the intake interview. The child was too young to be left in the waiting room so she joined us for the interview. As the mother and I talked the child played with some baby dolls I had. After a short time I became aware of the child's chattering to the dolls as she took care of them. However, I was not able to understand a word of what the child was saying. The speech of a 3-year-old should be clear enough for a person outside the immediate family to understand with little difficulty. When I asked the mother whether she could understand the child, she said that no one could understand her speech. While I worked with the mother regarding her concerns about the child and her parenting skills, the child was referred to a speech and language pathologist for evaluation.

The information obtained during these two interviews as a result of the children's fortuitous presence would not have been immediately available had they been excluded from the session. However, the information would have been presented within the first session or two in my work with the child. To reiterate, preference and circumstances often determine how the therapist deals with initial contacts with a family in conflict. Whatever the approach, useful information is obtained that will help the therapist understand the nature of the family's dilemma.

Adolescents are handled differently. I first see the parents and the teenager together, then just the teenager, and then the family again. In this way I establish the boundaries between the adolescent, myself, and the parents.

> Mr. and Mrs. C. contacted me regarding the "acting out" behaviors of their 13-year-old daughter, Jane. During the intake Mrs. C. did most of the talking. Mr. C. deferred to his wife while Jane made faces or nodded her head in agreement, but would not otherwise take part in the discussion. After about half an hour, I asked the parents to leave, and I continued my intake with Jane. She was then much more open and forthcoming about the issues that were bothering her. When the parents returned, I explained that if I were to see Jane, my primary commitment was to her. This meant that I would not talk with either of them without Jane's explicit permission or presence and that should they call, I would inform Jane about their communication with me. Further, I would not share with them my communications with Jane. They were accepting of my therapeutic limits and treatment began.

Adolescents need separation from their parents and privacy to develop a trusting relationship with a helping adult. By affirming my commitment to the youngster, along with the exclusion of her parents, I have taken the first steps in developing a viable, working relationship.

Many therapists discuss the necessity for establishing one's authority with parents at the first contact by stipulating and adhering to specific goals and ideals. The authority of the therapist, however, develops over time and through her demonstration of competence as a person who understands people in general and the clients specifically. It takes time and does not need arbitrary adherence to specific guidelines (Sullivan 1953).

There are other realities that need to be considered at this initial therapeutic step. The therapist is a stranger, albeit someone who may be helpful to the parents. They must decide whether or not to place the care of their child into the hands of this stranger. I would seriously question the motivation and investment of middle-class parents if they did not interview the therapist to find out what kind of person she is. While some therapists may view this as the parents' resistance to the therapeutic process, it is a legitimate and realistic concern of parents and should be addressed directly during the intake interview.

Lower-class parents often seem to respond as though they have little control regarding the intake or therapeutic processes. In this instance it is the responsibility of the therapist to raise these issues for the parents and help them to ask questions about the therapist, the evaluation, and the therapeutic process, and to gain answers to their unasked questions.

We have considered all of these factors and set up an appointment time to meet. We meet the parents in the waiting room, observing all along. How do we introduce ourselves? My preference is to begin this initial session formally, as one would expect between strangers, using Dr., Mr., and Mrs. forms of address. The use of first names may come in time as a working or cooperative relationship is formed. This formality sets boundaries in place, an important aspect of the therapeutic process, even with children.

I note how the family members arrange themselves in the office and who initiates the conversation.

> A couple entered my office with the wife moving toward one of a set of chairs I had pointed out while her husband wanted to sit in my chair, which was placed by itself. Initial hypothesizing about this behavior included the possibility of a rift in the marital relationship: having to fend off two females and needing protection and to be in charge.

As it happened, the mother took charge of the session and proceeded to talk about the child's problems in such a manner as to prevent either the child's father or myself from responding. Needless to say, treatment was not initiated by this family.

Observation gives the therapist a great deal of information about current behavior. But we wish to obtain information that will clarify the history of the family as an autonomous unit. In addition, a history of the parents will help us understand what the parents bring from their families of origin to their current family.

These are some of the concerns and needs of the therapist. What about the needs of the parents? Initially, they are probably anxious about telling the therapist their story. In helping the family begin I usually ask, "How can I help you?" In this manner parents can maintain control and they can begin where they feel most comfortable; they are not being led by an authority into uncomfortable areas. This approach also aids in the establishment of a cooperative partnership should a therapeutic relationship develop. Furthermore, the discussion of the parents' understanding of the problems enables the therapist to begin to hypothesize about possible intervention strategies to help the parents help their child. Throughout, the therapist is observing both parents and how they respond to each other and to the interviewer.

An in-depth developmental history of the child, beginning with the pregnancy should include behavior, physical development, and emotional and social development. (Appendix A is a sample intake as well as an intake interview that has been written in narrative form.)

If, during the intake interview, I have seen the child in his interactions with parents, a beginning picture of the child's functioning within the family can be obtained. However, the problem is defined by the parents from their perspective, not from the child's. Children can neither fight against parental perceptions nor articulate the difficulties they are experiencing. A complete diagnostic assessment based on psychological tests that tap a wide variety of domains is therefore an indispensable part of the evaluation of children to determine problems in living as experienced by the children themselves.

Earlier in this chapter I mentioned the reestablishment of the empathic bonds between children and their parents. This is an important outcome of the therapeutic work with children that helps them maintain the growth established as a result of treatment and helps them remain on a developmental par with peers. The establishment of a therapeutic environment in the home arises from an alliance between the therapist and the parents, enabling the parents to become co-therapists.

> Mrs. D. consulted me regarding her 6-year-old daughter, Julie, who has been unable to sleep the night through, in her own bed, because she is "scared." Mrs. D. stated that she does not have the same kind of connection with Julie as she has with her younger son and older daughter. As she described the differences in her feelings for the three children, she was able to say that this middle child of hers so reminded her of her own neediness as a child that she did not want to be in very much contact with Julie. When I suggested that she could not empathize with Julie, Mrs. D. readily agreed. She then proceeded to talk about how much Julie reminded her of herself that she had to push the child away for fear that her sense of abandonment by her parents would be so intense, she would slip into a life-threatening depression.

Therapy would help Mrs. D. resolve the difficulties that interfere with her responding to Julie empathically. This approach to the presenting problem assumes that the father has no role in the difficulties the child is exhibiting, and conceptualizes the difficulties as interpersonal and not as intrapsychic. However, this approach neither helps the mother understand how she affects her child nor explains the symptomatology the child is expressing. Mrs. D. and I worked for some months on what it is about Julie that interfered with Mrs. D.'s ability to respond to the child on a more empathic level. Further, recommendations for the mother's own treatment were also made and accepted. Between the mother's therapy and my interventions with her in terms of parenting, Julie began to have her needs met. As Ornstein (1976) has suggested, "The enhancement or creation of parental empathy is central to the treatment of children, and . . . this objective is best achieved when the meaning of the child's symptoms is translated into behavioral terms to his immediate emotional environment" (p. 27).

Ornstein further states that the development of an empathic bond creates a therapeutic milieu in the home that allows for the completion of developmental tasks that had been interfered with. In this way, too, the parents become part of the therapeutic endeavor with the child and are less likely to sabotage the treatment of the child, which enhances the therapy in the long run. The initial intake is often a therapeutic contact for the parents seeking help. It is here that the stage can be set to help the parents regain the empathic responses they have lost as the child has grown and matured.

2

BEGINNING
PSYCHOTHERAPY

The beginning of psychotherapy is a natural evolution of the process begun with the first telephone contact. When I have done the psychological assessment, meeting the child in the waiting room becomes an extension of the processes already established. If I have met only the parents previously, I greet them first, for it is with them that I have established a beginning relationship, and then I introduce myself to the child.

I usually shake hands with the school-age child and invite her to my playroom. I assume the child of this age can adequately separate from her parent. When greeting the preschooler I usually squat so as to be on eye level and also shake hands, asking the child to come with me to my playroom, and inviting parents in for the first session. I expect a child of this age to have difficulties separating until she feels comfortable with me. Thus, the first issue in the treatment of a preschool child is usually one of separation, while for the school-age child it is one of making contact and communicating.

At some point during the first two sessions, preferably the first, the reason the child is being seen must be discussed. This discussion includes the child's major problems and information about therapy, such as time and length of sessions. According to Brooks (1985):

> The dangers of not discussing with children during the first couple of sessions (preferably the initial session) why they are seeing a therapist is to enter into a complicity of silence that reinforces the belief that their problems are too painful (shameful, embarrassing) to discuss; this silence also compromises the setting of treatment goals. [pp. 762–763]

FIRST SESSIONS

During the first session, the fears and anxieties of the child as well as of the parents set off reactions that enable the therapist to see the characteristic modes of functioning parents and child use when dealing with stressful feelings and situations. The behaviors we observe are the child's response to her own feelings, which propels her into the therapeutic relationship. In this way the child becomes an active participant in the treatment process. As the therapist responds, the child learns that the therapist is interested in and identified with the child. The following is an example of an initial therapy session in which the therapist does not respond to the communications of the child.

> Sandy, a 6-year-old girl, the product of a rape, had been rejected by her mother. But guilt had prevented the mother from giving up Sandy for adoption, even though she had considered it. The child had been raised with strictness and high expectations. Behaviors the mother considered deviant were rigidly punished as they raised the mother's anxiety regarding the possibility of Sandy having inherited "bad genes" from her natural father, who was in jail for the rape of a number of young girls. There is a younger, much preferred half-brother. Sandy was brought to the center by her stepfather who seemed to give Sandy warmth and acceptance. When she was met

by the therapist she seemed apprehensive, yet the separation from the stepfather occurred without any difficulty. In the playroom Sandy was told that the hour was set aside just for her, and that she could do whatever she wanted in the room and during the time allotted. The therapist (a young woman in her second year of graduate school) pointed out where the toys were located and indicated that Sandy had complete access to them. After this brief introduction to the playroom, Sandy took a seat at the table. She said nothing and she did not give any indication of wanting to do anything. This child, with her rigid upbringing, seemed unable to function without specific direction. Sandy then began to stare at the dolls. Even as the child did not have the internal freedom to act overtly, she did communicate what she would like to do, which the therapist noted and articulated: the therapist asked Sandy if she would like to play with the dolls. The question was interpreted by the child as permission to act. Sandy selected the biggest doll and spent considerable time brushing her hair. When asked if she was going to name the doll, there was no response. The therapist, looking for a verbal interaction with the child, overlooked the child's real inability to play, which required comment. The therapist also picked out a doll in the hope of eliciting interaction through this medium, but Sandy made no attempts to reciprocate.

It would seem that the therapist's own anxiety about the lack of verbalization interfered with her ability to either identify with the child or to respond to the feelings being expressed nonverbally. Fortunately, the therapist recovered and wondered whether such attempts to play with Sandy allowed her the freedom that had been promised to her in this room. Perhaps Sandy did not want to play. The therapist decided to back off.

> There were a few moments of puzzled silence and inactivity on Sandy's part. Then on her own, the child began to search the drawers for something to play with. After a few minutes she proclaimed that there was nothing there and with a look of boredom and a sigh sat down again and began to draw.

It is possible the child was angry with the therapist's intrusion and let her know that what was in the playroom was not acceptable, the therapist included. She then became involved in an activity, drawing quietly, that not only emphasized the fact that she was a good little girl, but also allowed her to avoid contact with the therapist, who had not responded to her unverbalized feelings.

This therapy session points out a major problem most beginning therapists encounter with their child clients. Therapists are trained in the "talking cure" model of psychotherapy. When there is no talk, we are often at a loss as to what to do. According to Ekstein (1966), there is a variety of modes of communication with children. The three most important are language, play, and enactment.

As one initiates linguistic communication with a child, the cognitive level of functioning and the language level of development must be considered. The therapist's language must be altered to match the child's level. This matching helps the development of a therapeutic alliance through which the work of therapy can proceed.

Play is another form of communication the therapist must master. Each child uses her own play metaphors to communicate unconscious conflicts. Development and the issues of each stage must be thoroughly understood to enable a connection to be made between the play theme being enacted and the developmental eras that gave rise to it.

Enactment is the direct behavioral expression of the issues a child attempts to grapple with. This usually occurs when the child can neither play out the issue symbolically nor express it verbally. This is a rather primitive way of telling the therapist about the issues the child is struggling to resolve.

Jim, a 10-year-old boy with severe reading difficulties and a great deal of pent-up rage directed toward his uninvolved father, was seen by a male therapist. During the initial session he built a structure with dominoes, announcing that if he didn't destroy the building within three tries the enemy would win. The therapist noted that when the blocks refused to topple over he would then add more blocks adjacent to it in an attempt to create a weak spot so that it would fall down. Much ambivalence was being expressed in the child's behavior; even though he wanted to win, he was also afraid to do so. After a period of time the well-constructed edifice toppled to the floor with a sigh of relief from both Jim and the therapist.

Throughout this interplay there was a great deal of tension in the behavior of the child, which was relieved when he finally knocked the building down. Jim was able to leave the dominoes and look over the other toys, continually touching the boxing gloves but neither picking them up nor talking about them. This tied in very well with his need to express his angry feelings and his inability to do so except through some form of enactment. A great deal happened and was communicated in this session; however, it was seen rather than heard.

REFUSALS

Some school-aged children refuse to separate from the parents. There are many conflicting opinions as to how to handle this situation. Some therapists force the child to come with her, some let the parents handle the situation and wait for the resolution, some invite the parents to come into the office but ask the parents to remain standing, forcing them to separate from the child. My own handling of this situation depends on all the information I have obtained so far from the intake, assessment, and initial contact with the child. However, I assume the child as well as the parent have difficulty in separating. As a consequence, I might have the first few sessions in the waiting room with both parent and child, or I might have both parent and child come into the playroom and work with them there. No matter the approach, the therapeutic process begins at the point of contact between myself and the client(s). I am alert to the verbal and nonverbal messages being communicated. Talking with all the parties, establishing rapport, and understanding the feelings of all concerned are part of the process of working toward the separation of parent and child, which becomes the first task of the treatment. Parents and child need support and understanding in this anxiety-producing situation, which will eventually alter existing patterns of interacting and relating. Changing and being different are frightening and difficult, and demand much courage.

The parents need help in tolerating the anxiety of the separation and finally leaving the playroom. The child may need to visit the waiting room for reassurance that the parents are still there. For the younger child, this anxiety and the necessity for reassurance are appropriate. For the older child, they are inappropriate and indicate problems in separation.

The child's refusal to come to the playroom arouses much anxiety in the child, the parents, and the therapist. However, the refusal can be used to help the child understand why she is there, that although she is afraid of growing up, her parents are also having a difficult time letting the child grow up. That both the child and the parents have a similar problem helps take the full burden of difficulty from the shoulders of the child.

INTRODUCTION TO TREATMENT

The first session is a tense one, both for the child and the therapist; the child is seeing a therapist because the parents are worried about the behaviors and problems the child is exhibiting. The therapist communicates this information to the child in language appropriate to the child's cognitive level. The information obtained from the psychological assessment of the child is summarized in this first communication. The therapeutic process is described simply; for example, the therapist and the child are going to be seeing each other at 4 o'clock every Wednesday in the playroom because of all the concerns that have been talked about, and although talking about secret worries is very hard, talking helps to make things better. And because talking to a stranger about secret matters is hard, for the time being the two of you will concentrate on getting to know one another.

THE THERAPEUTIC RELATIONSHIP

The activities and verbalizations of the child are influenced and may be determined by the therapist's presence in this unique setting and situation. Whatever the child does or says conveys to a considerable degree her feelings about herself and the immediate situation. Beginning where the child is and dealing directly and immediately with the feelings and thoughts being expressed is more crucial than dealing with the so-called problems that brought the child into therapy. If the therapy is child-centered, then whatever reactions the child brings can be used to aid the child in achieving a new sense of herself. However, this new sense of the self occurs within the context of an experience in living in the here and now. The therapist cannot establish a relationship with a child who does nothing, just as a child cannot find a connection with a therapist who is inactive. The child needs a real person.

Catering to the needs and wants of the child as a means of "making up" for what the parents are not giving the child prevents the child from expressing more immediate negative feelings. If the child owes you something because you have been so nice and kind, how can the child ever be angry? She would be ungrateful and then lose what little was gained from the relationship. Too active and continuous a participation in the actual play of the child by the therapist does not help the child deal with her dilemmas in living. A balance between activity and passivity must be maintained by the therapist. The therapist and child will set the parameters for activity-passivity. The major responsibility of the therapist lies in helping the child to do what she is free or ready to do without trying to force the child into any particular channel of expression.

TREATMENT OF THE PRESCHOOL CHILD

Flapan and Neubauer (1972) suggest that the preschool child often brings specific features to the beginning phase of treatment that makes the establishment of the therapeutic alliance a rather complex undertaking. The child's dependency on the parent, limited ability for self observation, and wishful thinking are among characteristics that make the development of a working alliance difficult. In addition, it takes a great deal of work to help the child better understand her world. The therapy session may be the first time that the child is meeting an adult who is willing to listen and hear her, who has the patience to wait, and who permits the child to follow her thoughts and feelings—in short, someone who does not give directions. But the child is also responding to the newness of the situation, and what the therapist observes may not be typical of the child's pattern of responding. The younger the child, the stronger may be the initial reaction to the therapeutic situation.

Some children are unable to separate from the mother. (A certain amount of clinging behavior is expected in children under 5.) These children may not have completely worked through separation-individuation, or the clinging may be manifestations of anger and manipulation on the part of the child.

Excessive clinging after the first few contacts, however, is of concern. In these cases, the mother often has to be present in the treatment room until the child is later able to separate. Her presence has obvious implications for the beginning phase of treatment. To untie the child from the mother may be a central issue, involving an understanding of many unconscious feelings and conflicts that need to be interpreted to both mother and child. It may well be that the therapist's first task is to help the mother achieve separation so that therapy may progress.

When working with preschool children, the beginning phase progresses much sooner to the middle phase than with other age groups, because the therapeutic relationship is often set up on a parent–child model, thus serving the child's dependency and security needs (Klein 1975). Despite the many differences between child and adult therapy, the therapeutic goals are the same, that is, to bring about the resolution of conflicts, to enable the child to grow, and to make it possible to proceed where there had been interference with and fixation of the development. Anna Freud (1965a) suggested that it is especially important for a positive relationship to develop between child and therapist. She pointed out that adults can tolerate periods of negative feelings, but negative feelings directed against the therapist by the child are disruptive to the therapeutic process. However, a more basic problem in child therapy is that the child's parents are real and present. They are not the remembered love objects of adult patients. The therapist, therefore, enters the child's world as a new person and will probably share with the parents the child's love and hate.

Near the beginning of the session, 4-year-old Connie went to the bathroom, leaving the door open, and said I could come with her. She sat on the toilet singing so loudly it echoed off the tile walls and around the clinic. When she was finished we raced back to the room, where Connie picked up a naked adult female doll. She began yelling at the doll calling it bad and saying no. She picked up a plastic knife and began "cutting" up the doll, even trying to pull the arms and legs off. She then began stabbing it in the stomach all the while calling it bad and yelling at it. She then put some brown clay on it, calling it blood and saying that the cat bit it. I suggested she might be angry with the doll, which had no impact on her behavior; in fact, she went on to spank the doll with paints. Until this session I had thought that she was angry with me because of the psychological testing I was doing. However, I speculated that she had been displacing onto me her angry feelings that belonged to her mother. This could be why Mrs. M. related that Connie had been well behaved both at home and in nursery school since the testing began.

The above vignette illustrates the child's inclusion of the therapist under the umbrella of feelings related to the mother. However, the sessions have assumed much of the child's negative feelings, thereby freeing her up and allowing her to function more appropriately than previously. Unfortunately, this phenomenon is often misperceived by the parents as a resolution of the difficulties that motivated them to seek help in the first place. This misperception can result in an interrupted treatment. An ongoing relationship with the parents that fosters a partnership between therapist and parents often circumvents the precipitous withdrawal of the child from therapy.

TREATMENT OF THE SCHOOL-AGE OR LATENCY CHILD

The problems in doing therapy with the latency child (ages 6 to 12) differ from those encountered with the preschooler or the teenager. The normal style of "pathological-like" behavior, such as whining, supersensitivity, general unhappiness, the development of tics, and other such behaviors, makes the child difficult to evaluate. The child's style of communication, for example, babbling on and on, playing out fantasy after fantasy, and jumping from one developmental level to another without warning, is foreign to the adult. While there is disagreement on how to treat latency children, there are some guidelines that will be discussed below. Children can fall along a continuum of behavior, which is described by Sarnoff (1976). At one extreme is the "overdefiant" child, who fills up time with constant superficial chatter, reluctant to engage with the therapist. At the other extreme is the "overcompliant" child, who spends much of the time in fantasy to the exclusion of interacting with the therapist. Both types of child often ignore or deny the verbal interventions of the therapist.

There is another therapy problem specific to the treatment of latency children that Sarnoff calls "lulling." It is a therapist's blocking or altering of attention to the therapy situation as the child repetitively plays out the same fantasy. The danger of lulling lies in its lack of attention to subtle changes in the fantasy. Some examples of lulling include passively watching the child play, becoming over-involved in playing or writing, and doodling during the session. Since the changes in fantasy are important to the therapy process, it is imperative that the therapist monitor herself and deal with the possibility of a personal conflict being involved.

Therapy with the latency-aged child is based on understanding typical latency behavior and helping the child to develop age-appropriate cognitive, affective, and defensive functioning. An attempt is made in the treatment to help the child develop skills to handle the aggression and excitement that are prominent symptoms of this age and allow the use of fantasy and education to grow.

> George, a 9-year-old, was referred because of aggressive, acting out behavior at school and at home. His parents refused to be involved in any form of therapy, but nevertheless did not interfere with George's therapy. During the first sessions, George was immediately attracted to some "hot wheels" but said that he couldn't play with them because in order for them to run on the tracks they needed a booster, which was missing. He then began to build an elaborate track out of the available blocks and soldiers and trucks. As he was quietly building, his back was facing the therapist as if he had forgotten that anyone else was present. The therapist seated herself at the table and began to paint but it was doubtful that George was aware of it. Only after the therapist began to work with a puzzle did George occasionally look at her out of the corner of his eye as he continued to build. The therapist said, "I feel left out and it doesn't feel good." George said, "I know, I have felt left out a lot of times," and continued to play by himself. The therapist continued, "You apparently don't care that I feel left out because you're still playing by yourself." He sarcastically replied, "Well, if you want me to be polite, I should ask you to please come and play with me." After he was told he didn't have to be polite, he appeared shocked.

She then commented that maybe he felt more comfortable in playing by himself because he didn't know her. He didn't respond. She began to ask him about his track and the soldiers. He seemed quite willing to talk about it and explained that it was a military mission. The truck has to be loaded with explosives that the soldiers were carrying. After the truck is loaded, it has to go all around the track and under the bridge. The therapist said, "That's an awfully dangerous mission, isn't it?" George agreed. She added, "Those men must be afraid to carry the explosives. They need to help each other. A lot of times we can't do something alone so we need help." George said, "I guess so."

This vignette suggests the child's need for control as well as a need to be alone. Furthermore, it points to the necessity of treating children with dignity and respect, which can then result in a sense of cooperation and working together rather than at cross-purposes.

The vignette also indicates the anger and hurt this boy has experienced at the hands of adults, for example, the danger inherent in the carrying of explosives as well as politeness as socially approved ways of functioning. George also communicated information that he had to function appropriately irrespective of his feelings, and furthermore, he could do what he wished only when isolated from other people. The therapist communicated to George that socially appropriate behavior was not crucial to her, which allowed George to respond to her interventions.

Although the latency child is in a state of psychological upheaval, there is often an outward expression of calm pliability and educability, which serves to mask the internal struggles taking place and keeps the adult at a distance. The child feels that she must maintain control over affects. This control, which has only been recently accomplished, is experienced as fragile. While a latency child might appear to be very agreeable, it is probable that anger, resentment, fear, and anxiety are just under the surface, constantly pushing against the child's hard-won controls.

During middle childhood, the active fantasies that were so much in evidence during the early years are less easily elicited. Nevertheless, they are still present, but in a more disguised manner. The child is more reality oriented, hence the emphasis on rules. The high interest in board games is the symbolic expression of the interest in and need for controls. The competition of the games allows the child to express in a socially appropriate manner the aggression that is common during this stage of development. However, playing board games during the therapeutic hour has two major pitfalls: (1) verbal interchange may be limited; and (2) the greater skill of the therapist in strategy and game playing means the child may lose, but allowing the child to win is not real.

Limited verbal interchange is usually a resistance by both the therapist and the child to the development of the therapeutic relationship. However, game–playing behavior has meanings that need to be understood so that we are better able to respond to the feelings, defenses, and conflicts it expresses.

> Maria, 9 years old, was the youngest child in an Italian Catholic family. She was in therapy because of fearfulness that resulted in her occasional refusal to go to school. During the course of her two years in therapy, Sorry was the game that was most often played. Initially, she was a timid player, refusing to send her therapist's marker back to start, thus losing the games deliberately. Her game behavior indicated to the therapist that she was afraid of her aggressive/assertive impulses. She avoided coming to grips with the major task of the developmental era: the establishment of her competence as an individual separate from her family. Her therapist remarked on her game-playing behavior and they discussed her fear of winning.

At termination, Maria exhibited a great deal of animation and enjoyment of the game. She readily sent her therapist's markers back to start and used strategies that enabled her to win consistently. Her

aggressive/assertive impulses, which had been appropriately integrated by this time, were now expressed in her involvement in a
wide range of activities that challenged her competency and enabled
her to prove her increasing abilities to herself. Academically, she
was also doing better, and peer relationships had developed.

Game Playing in Latency

Games as well as activities in which there is rivalry give legitimate
outlet to aggressive and exhibitionistic impulses that can no longer
be expressed as directly as in early childhood. Games of chance have
two major symbolic features:

1. winning—enacting wishes to steal and displace, exploit and
   triumph
2. losing—feeling robbed, cheated, and punished.

How should the therapist play a board game is a question that
arises repeatedly during the course of treatment. Should the therapist allow the child to win or should the therapist play to win? There
are both reality and therapeutic issues embedded in this question.
Reality considerations include:

1. the therapist is a better game player than the child
2. the child will be aware of the therapist's allowing the child
   to win
3. the therapist has a need to win and best her opponent.

The child will expect the adult to win games. Losses are impactful
only when the child can't win in the contest with the adult. If the
adult gives herself a handicap, to even the odds, and shares the rea-
soning with the youngster, the playing field is leveled and the child
can begin to learn about fairness and feeling potent via the process of
game playing and not just in the winning or losing of the game.

The therapeutic issues are clarified when winning and losing are not so prominent in the game playing. These issues center upon the child's feelings of competence, competition, and a variety of other feelings that need to be dealt with interpersonally. The strategies the child uses during the game often provide the therapist with glimpses into interpersonal negotiations and resolution of conflict.

Providing false experiences undermines the therapeutic adventure and thereby lessens its impactfulness. Being real and setting an example are important ways of functioning with the child and teach her important lessons about how adults in their interactions with children can be. Thus at the end of a game the child is able to reassure herself that the results have been achieved solely by the rules and luck of the game.

Sometimes the child may be unable to communicate through either language or play, but may be able to express the conflict through more primitive forms of acting out. Simon, a 10-year-old with a history of aggressive acting out both at home and at school, was being seen by his second therapist in two years (his first therapist had moved). The new therapist reported the first session with Simon:

> Simon quickly left his mother's side and was in the playroom before I could get there. Once in the playroom he seemed familiar with the setting and quickly chose the toy he wished to play with: a set of wooden train tracks with an accompanying train also made of wood. While assembling the toy, Simon spoke of how he remembered me from the previous year at [one of the neighborhood schools] as "Teach" and of all the things he and Jim [his previous therapist] had done last year. Throughout the play session, he made reference to all the things he was permitted to do with Jim.

This form of verbalization is known as signal communication: the child is inviting a response, a discussion, an answer to what he is saying. The therapist's response to Simon is not noted in the record;

however, that he was not responsive to the feelings expressed by the child is clear from the following play sequences.

> After colliding the train into the wall and running it off the tracks a few times, all expressive of his angry feelings, Simon decided to play ringtoss. When he lost the match, he became more angry. He showed me a dollar bill that his mother gave him, expressed how Jim had permitted him to go to the student union for candy bars, and asked if we could go. It was apparent that by losing the game he was also losing some control in this situation, so I agreed.

The therapist missed the significance of the behavior, in that by losing the game, Simon confirmed what he felt about himself, that he was a loser and therefore needed a concession from the therapist to be a winner. His mother, unable to respond to his needs, left him feeling rejected and so had his previous therapist. The symbolic nature of the play came too close to reality as he experienced it and therefore Simon needed to get away from the situation. The therapist supported the acting out by not dealing with the material. The acting-out behavior of the child also angered the therapist and thereby rendered him incapable of dealing with the material the child was presenting. The child enacting his anger and fury at being rejected also served to keep the new therapist at bay and prevent him from responding to the hurt of the child with his strong underlying need for comfort and succor.

Jimmy, an 8-year-old, has strong feelings about his experienced rejection by his mother and by his previous therapist. He is described, by a male therapist:

> Jimmy arrived at the center shortly before 6:00 and was busy looking at the children's books in the waiting room when I approached him and introduced myself to him. His only response was, "Oh." As we headed for the playroom Jimmy told me of how he had been coming to the center for two years, that I was the third person he had seen, and that he used the playroom upstairs. He also inquired

if I were seeing anyone else to which I replied no. Immediately upon entering the playroom he picked up the darts and began to throw them at the door. While doing so, a conversation about having a different therapist was initiated and how sometimes it is hard to say good-bye to a person you get to know. Jimmy seemed to accept this and stated that he did find it hard, especially when he likes the person. He then changed his attention from the darts and our conversation to the building blocks and began to make a tanker truck. As he was building this, he spoke of his erector set and, as described in the therapy summaries of the previous therapist, gave an in-depth explanation of diesel engines and heavy machinery. When I said that at one time I had driven a tanker truck, Jimmy seemed quite surprised and for the first time looked directly at me. He quickly returned his attention to his truck building and engine explanations in what seemed to be an attempt to shut me out of his activity. Determined not to be shut out, I began to "assist" Jimmy in his productions by holding and sometimes handing him his needed materials for construction. During this time Jimmy mentioned that sometimes "I can't do anything right" and it was noticed that he was having difficulty assembling a truck according to the diagram. I reflected the statement and added, "It could be frustrating when that happens," which appeared to spark more conversation about frustrations and individual limitations on performance, with Jimmy adding that it also was "annoying, but people shouldn't be expected to do everything well." Throughout our conversations Jimmy continually referred only to himself, "I am . . . , I will . . . , I can. . . ." At one point, and quite unexpectedly, Jimmy said, "What can we build next?" and we decided to build a house. The remainder of the session was spent constructing a house with me assisting the "head engineer." When Jimmy was told there were ten minutes left in this session, he ceased building the house, went to the shelf and found a gun, and began to shoot the toys on the shelf. Not giving me time to reflect on this action, he put the gun down and took out a toy police car from his pocket, apparently brought with him from home, stating that he "liked police cars." At the end of the session, Jimmy was asked if he would like to clean up the toys he had used. He responded yes, but then did not do anything. He then stated that they could be left "for the person who cleans up." He picked up the house that we had been building and placed it on a high shelf, stating that he wanted it to be saved for next week when we came back to see each other again. Jimmy was then taken up to the center and returned to his parents.

During this therapy session, the therapist responded to the behaviors of the child, which then allowed the child to begin to establish a relationship with the therapist.

Simon and Jimmy engaged in some minimal play, which is characteristic of 9- to 12-year-olds. The amount of fantasy a child during the middle childhood years expresses is dependent on the environment, but generally is much less than during the preschool years. There seems to be an unconscious drive toward the repression of fantasy. However, with our emphasis on achievement and learning along with the demands of school, it is not clear that there is really an unconscious drive toward the repression of fantasy. Because of a variety of sociocultural factors, the child might repress or at least suppress fantasy expression. Children who come from families where imagination, fantasy, and make-believe are cherished activities might fantasize comfortably, but in the privacy of their own rooms, not in the presence of adults. Thus, fantasy has the potentiality of remaining a viable modality for the child for far longer than the preschool years if this activity is valued.

PROBLEMS IN WORKING THERAPEUTICALLY WITH CHILDREN

There are basic problems encountered in working with young people:

1. Since the child does not enter therapy on her own and makes no contact with the therapist, she does not have to abide by the rules of therapy.

2. Since the child does not take any long-term view of any situation, the discomforts, strain, and anxiety caused by treatment in the present weigh more heavily than the idea of future gains.
3. The child acts in preference to talking; behaviors dominate the therapy.
4. The child feels more threatened by therapy than the adult and defenses are kept more rigidly.
5. Since all children tend to externalize their inner conflicts in the form of battles with the environment, they look for environmental solutions in preference to internal changes.

Different age levels express these problems in ways specific to the developmental level. The preschool child expresses her resistance to therapy most effectively and pointedly by refusing to be separated from the parents, or by crying, throwing temper tantrums, closing one's eyes, and making the therapist go away.

The school-age child usually cannot remember what the parents said about coming into therapy, and exhibits no real anxiety about parental complaints, as the complaints are the parents' and not the child's. The child therefore wonders why she is seeing a therapist and asks if is she crazy. The school-age child is embarrassed to talk about things that must not be mentioned. She is concerned about what other kids will say. Will the therapist question the child about these unmentionables? Will the child be teased? Can the therapist read minds? The child will not tell the therapist about a difficult situation even when it is conscious and remembered. The child cannot be sure the therapist won't tell the parents about the bad things she does, or when sure of the therapist, the child may be caught between mixed loyalties to the parents and therapist. The child may be pulled to tell the therapist yet needs to protect the parents from the secret at the same time.

The prepubescent child (ages 10 to 12) exhibits the same resistance as the younger child (ages 6 to 10) with some additional features. She needs to be constantly doing something; activity binds anxiety for the child. Resistances are conscious and the child is aware of and uses them deliberately.

Children of all ages are concerned that talking about their fears will bring them on. If this occurs, (1) they will not be able to cope with them, or (2) the fears that now come only at night will also happen during the day and then they will have no relief from them.

The emotions of a child in developmental difficulties are diffuse, undifferentiated, and generally negative at the beginning of therapy. The child is frightened and angry, expressing these feelings generally. The child may also be afraid of almost everything and everybody, leading to wishes to be left alone. The greater the child's trust in the therapist and the greater the feelings of acceptance and respect, the more focused feeling can become and then be resolved.

THERAPY STRATEGIES

Therapy strategies abound for intervention in childhood problems. Play is the most commonly used therapeutic vehicle with children. Therapy cannot be effective without a relationship, which begins with an interaction. The communication between child and therapist initiates the working relationship and stamps the therapeutic process with uniqueness for both child and therapist. The working alliance becomes possible when the therapist responds with understanding, sensitivity, and acceptance to the child's communication.

> When I met 9-year-old Brian for the first time he lay down on the floor pretending he was asleep. His mother's efforts to get him to "stop fooling around" and go with me were to no avail. Reassuring the mother that Brian would join me when he felt more comfortable enabled the child to get up and come with me to the playroom. Once inside he immediately picked up a gun, pointed it at me, and

said, "Bang!" I commented, "If I were not here, you wouldn't have to be either." Brian smiled, put the gun down, and began exploring the room and commenting about the toys and what he liked to play with.

My comment alleviated Brian's initial refusal, allowing him to begin, to become involved in the therapeutic process; my intervention in the playroom allowed the session to flow.

Typically, the therapist reacts to those parts of the session that are most intense and are repeated without alteration. The therapist's response helps the child resolve some dilemma she is trying to understand as well as informs the child that the therapist is with her. As the therapist and child work together, the relationship develops and deepens. Patterns of behavior are clarified and with it comes the possibility of providing clearer and more effective interventions. These interpretations provide for the continuity of the material from hour to hour, from present to the past, and from person to person. Since the therapeutic relationship embodies the elements of a living experience, feelings are an essential part of that relationship. The therapist is in a position to identify affects the child is both willing and unwilling to experience and to explore them. The source of the child's fantasy and play arises from her relationships, needs, affects, and present troubling events.

TREATMENT ISSUES

We are strangers to the child, even if we have had prior contacts. Each of the previous sessions with the child had its well-defined limits. If the child was at the intake, the parents did most of the talking and explaining. If questions were directed at the child that she did not wish to deal with, one of the parents was sure to come to the child's aid. During the testing the child was asked to deal with many different kinds of tasks that had their own inherent limits; the child somehow knew how much to give or withhold throughout the testing. The first psychotherapy session is quite different, not only from the other sessions but from other adult encounters.

The therapist usually opens the session and symbolically gives something to the child. The understanding and recognition of the feelings the child must inevitably be experiencing is the most appropriate gift the therapist can give. Children do not know that the therapist is different from all other adults in their life. Sharing this information will have little impact on the child; however, enabling the child to experience this difference is the crucial factor. But the child can only experience the difference when the therapist acts.

> Eight-year-old Roger was referred for treatment because he was generally unhappy and was learning disabled. He came into the playroom and sat on the chair waiting for the therapist to do or say something. Mother had commented on the troubles he was having in school during the intake and had pinpointed the teacher's insensitivity to Roger as part of the problem. I used this information and suggested that it must be difficult to go to school when he had trouble learning and especially when the teacher did not understand. He brightened, got up, and began punching the punching bag as he related one instance after another of how unfair this teacher had been to him. Over the next 4 weeks we did an assessment, talked about how angry he was in school, and he punched on the punching bag. I received a call from the mother after the fourth session asking me what I had done to her son. In exploring the issues behind the question she was finally able to say that Roger has been acting like his old self and she was pleased to have him back.

The gift of being understood and accepted allowed Roger to begin to trust the therapist as a different kind of adult and to further elaborate on harmful experiences, expressing the anger that was associated with them. Roger was also freed up enough to function in a more relaxed, competent manner outside treatment.

BASIC PRINCIPLES IN CHILD THERAPY

1. Accept the child where she or he is.
2. Tell the truth.
3. Be alert to the feeling level of the child.
4. Maintain a deep respect for the child.
5. The child leads and the therapist follows. There should be no attempt to direct the child's actions or conversation.
6. The pacing of the therapy is the child's. The therapist does not hurry the therapy along.
7. The therapist sets realistic limits through which rapport is established.

The establishment of a therapeutic alliance with the child is dependent on clear limits that define the boundaries of the relationship between the therapist and the child. These limits promote the child's ability for reality testing. To permit a child to do whatever she wants is unrealistic and bears little relationship to what the child will meet in the world at large. To be effective, the therapy hour must not be so divorced from everyday life that there can be no carryover into the child's world outside the playroom. In addition, one cannot be sure that the child really wants what she says she wants. The child may simply be testing to see if the therapist can be manipulated, or if the therapist is strong enough to resist the manipulation and thereby provide the child with a sense of security. Limits are also important because if there are none it frightens the child. If it is not made abundantly clear that the therapist will protect the child against the destructive impulses that we all have, the child will feel guilty.

Limits are especially necessary for children who do not have sufficient internal controls. External controls support the child until the internal ones develop. Some of the limits for the playroom include:

1. The child cannot physically abuse the therapist.
2. Items cannot be deliberately destroyed.
3. Time limits should be adhered to.
4. The child stays within the room.

3

PLAY AND
THE SETTING FOR
CHILD THERAPY

Children use play to explore their universe, process their life experiences, test reality, express their thinking, develop role concepts and object relationships, and develop skills and strategies for problem solving. However, in spite of its significant role in development and in the resolution of emotional sticking points, play has often been seen as an unimportant activity engaged in when there is nothing else to do or when adults cannot attend to the needs and demands of the child. Because play is so crucial to adequate development, this chapter discusses the nature of play. Understanding the nature of play helps us understand why therapy with children must be conducted in a specific setting with toys that allow children to communicate their needs, feelings, and areas of conflict. Play is the expressive medium of the child, just as words are the medium of the adult. Children generally do not possess the vocabulary, the symbolism, the concepts, or the cognitive structures to express what it is that distresses them. The use of toys and play facilitates the expression of thoughts and feelings.

THEORIES OF PLAY

According to Singer (1973) there are a number of different theories of play:

1. Play is surplus energy. Because children do not have the responsibility of work, they find outlets for their excess energy in play.
2. Instinct, recapitulation, and cultural theories: children need to rid themselves of more primitive forms of behavior through play, which is related to the rituals of savages. Play helps them to work through these primitive forms so that they can become adequately functioning adults.

More recent theorizing about play has emphasized its role as a practice for later functioning (White 1959), but without the formal requirements of social behavior.

> Sandy, the mother of 4-year-old Jon, got into the car where the youngster was kneeling in the driver's seat wearing his father's hat, gloves, and scarf. He said, "Where do you want to go, Sandy?" Mother replied, "I don't know, you choose." Jon then said, "We'll go to the moon," and began turning the wheel to get there.

Psychoanalytic theories of play, such as those of Freud, Anna Freud, and Erikson, have viewed play as a substitute form of masturbation; an attempt to satisfy drives; an expression of wish-fulfilling tendencies; an attempt to resolve conflicts; an attempt to master, through repetition, situations of overwhelming anxiety; and an attempt to master reality.

Piaget (1952) thought play derived from the child's working out the two fundamental characteristics of experience and development: assimilation and accommodation. Further, he saw symbolic play, which is apparent from the age of 18 months onward, as being associated with assimilation rather than accommodation. Opie and Opie (1950, 1969, 1992), English ethologists and observers of children's play behavior, suggested that play has the qualities of exploration, mastery, and sheer enjoyment of fantasy in environments that are not well ordered or structured.

White (1959) saw play as an attempt to assimilate material that is novel to the child. Play is stimulating novelty, out of which learning develops, along with curiosity and the physical exploration of materials and objects. He further suggested that striving in children arises as part of the normal development of competence and that through play, children use their skills and abilities in an effective manner. Cognitive-affective theorists such as McClelland and colleagues (1953) and Tompkins (1963) have suggested that the imaginative play of children represents efforts to organize experiences and use motor and cognitive abilities to their fullest. Lichtenberg (1983) has suggested that children interact with novel material within their capacity for mastery. If material is presented too rapidly, before the child is able to assimilate effectively, he will be startled or even become frightened. If confronted with unassimilable and unfamiliar material over a prolonged period of time, a child will become angry and depressed. In either case, mastery cannot occur. Singer (1973) states, "Make-believe is a normal activity which is the outgrowth of the fundamental information processing of the child" (p. 199). Make-believe requires the following:

1. an opportunity for privacy and practice so that attention can be focused on internal activity
2. the availability of materials, such as stories told, experiences, playthings
3. freedom from interference by peers or adults who make demands for immediate motor/perceptual reactions
4. freedom from time commitments

5. the availability of adult models who encourage make-believe activity
6. cultural acceptance of privacy and make-believe.

Smilansky (1968), working with disadvantaged preschoolers in Israel, found that increasing sociodramatic play, play that enacts a story or theme, increased intellectual development. Lovinger (1974) found that by teaching children how to play, intellectual and verbal functioning increased. Research on the development of language has supported these findings (Bretherton 1984).

Smilansky (1968) described four types of play:

> *Functional play*: simple muscular activities that allow the child to practice and learn physical capabilities and to explore and experience the immediate environment;
>
> *Constructive play*: children learn the uses of various materials and can sustain play and concentrate for longer periods of time with a movement from exploration of material to making something;
>
> *Sociodramatic play*: symbolic in nature, expressing physical prowess, creative ability, and beginning social awareness;
>
> *Games with rules*: highest stage of play development, where the child accepts prearranged rules and adjusts to them, learning to control behavior, action, and reactions; there are strong elements of fantasy embedded within the game.

Thirteen-year-old Gerry was seen in a playroom because, like most young adolescents, he could not sustain a verbal therapeutic interaction. His play behaviors were almost exclusively of the games-with-rules kind, even though he did not engage his therapist in his games. Rather, Gerry talked to the therapist as he played his game. This youngster used one of the plastic bowling pins and a Nerf ball that were in the playroom. He explained how the various members of the National and American League baseball teams batted. As one listened it became apparent that there was an attempt to deal with the conflicts he was experiencing both at home and at school, but primarily he was trying to deal with issues of identification, recognition, and competence.

Paradoxically, make-believe relies heavily upon verbalization. In make-believe, the child must state what role he will take, the identity of an object in the play, what verbalizations the players will make, and what the play is about. In this manner, play enhances creativity, flexibility, intellectual growth, and social skills by helping the child unify scattered experiences while creating new combinations and ways of understanding those experiences. In addition, play pushes the child to draw on his experiences and knowledge through the playing of a role that demands intellectual discipline, judgment, perception, and selection. Through play the child learns to concentrate on a given theme, which leads to self-discipline and flexibility in his approach to various situations and other people's styles of functioning. These are abilities and capacities that therapists expect to find in individuals at the completion of treatment. During treatment play serves as the vehicle for the expression of thoughts, feelings, and developmental problem areas. Play is the child's communication to the therapist.

> Thirteen-year-old Matt had been repeatedly sodomized by a boyfriend of his mother. In the playroom he built a truck of Legos with long spears radiating from the back of the truck. Matt explained that when the truck was leaving and being pursued by aliens the spears could be shot out the back to protect the truck and the people inside from being hurt. When comments were made directly to him about the molestations, all he could do was hang his head and sit quietly as though he were not there. Through play Matt could talk about his fear of being hurt again even though he could not discuss his abuse directly. The therapist responded on that level. That is, she did not make a connection between the content of Matt's play and his abuse. Rather, she talked about how well the truck was able to protect and defend itself against attack. The value of play is its ability to circumvent the

permissiveness

child's reluctance to discuss issues directly and yet express these feelings and issues.

THE THERAPIST'S ROLE

The therapist's warmth and acceptance help children share their feelings, change, and grow.

> A 9-year-old boy announced at the beginning of a session, "Lovey, [a diminutive of my last name] you're an old fuck" to my negative response when he asked for some new toys. My spontaneous response, "You're not so hot either," took him by surprise. He probably expected me to berate him for his foul language. Not responding in the way in which he expected helped us move toward his anger with his mother who was always demanding that he be a good boy no matter what he felt. We could both be real and deal with what was real and important to this child.

This vignette demonstrates *permissiveness*, stating what one feels rather than enacting what one is feeling or replying in a socially pleasant manner. Permissiveness allows children to express their feelings in words or in play and to experiment with feelings that have been previously prohibited or inhibited. However, permissiveness is not license. Destruction of materials belonging to the playroom or to other clients is not allowed. Accidental damage does occur and should be responded to with acceptance, if it is truly inadvertent. As well, children may destroy their own productions such as paintings or models, and although this behavior can be delayed or interpreted, it should not be prevented. Rather, the therapist should respect the human dignity of the children with their strengths and limitations, permitting the children to be themselves. This acceptance is for the child, not the behavior. The therapist, through permissiveness and acceptance of the child, and the understanding gained through play, develops a relationship with the child that the child can use to release tension, develop maturity, better understand himself, share his fantasies, resolve his conflicts, and channel his energy in a more personally satisfying and socially acceptable manner.

At times unconscious conflicts may be resolved by repetition of play without verbalization by the child or interpretation by the therapist. At other times, depending on the individual child, the therapist may need to clarify and interpret what the child is feeling and experiencing. Play therapy uses the concepts of psychotherapy, including the principle that there is therapeutic value in the expression of hostility, and the reliving of past intrapsychic and environmentally caused traumatic experiences. While anger can be usefully discharged, rage should not receive unrestricted expression (Kernberg 1975) as it disorganizes the child's psychic organization.

Regression is a return to earlier, less mature behavior; it has a role in play therapy. It is a manifestation of more primitive behavior occurring after mature forms have been achieved. Regressive behavior can be an effort to repair psychic injury, to reroute a particular misdirected course.

Sometimes behavior that looks like regression in play is in fact a maturational lag. For example, a 12-year-old child who uses a peg-hammer toy may be merely servicing his need for eye-hand coordination.

> Seventeen-year-old Effie, who was diagnosed as having a nonverbal learning disability (difficulties with arithmetic, complex written material, and social interactions), asked to go to the playroom. Once there she looked for a card game to play. However, she had a great deal of difficulty scanning the playing field and could not win the game. She was quite discouraged and asked to play a different game. She was intrigued with Triominoes, which she played for many months. It was apparent that as she played this game her ability to scan the environment increased and she slowly began to win games. Her self-esteem slowly grew as well. Toward the end of one session she told me that she wanted to discuss the death of her dog during the next session. Her discussion the following week showed a maturity and depth that had not been present when we had begun working six

months previously. At that time she commented that I liked to go deep but she didn't. Now she did the depth work on her own.

Effie needed to face the developmental lag that has been interfering with her maturation. As she did so the growth in her verbal and interpersonal skills became evident.

A child bent on organizing or reorganizing his world uses opportunities to meet earlier frustrated needs. The play sessions provide the child the opportunity to try again. Regression and progression are often simultaneously desired and anxiety arousing to the child, who is thereby not "acting his age." The therapist, as well as the child, may naturally feel an aversion to regressed behavior. The smearing of brown finger paint is reminiscent of fecal smearing. The substitution of play for words is itself a recourse to an earlier mode of communication. The therapist may feel "left out," that the child is withdrawing from her, such as when a verbal child turns his back to the therapist and silently builds a house and breaks it down. The therapeutic session allows for regression, but the therapist does not encourage it because of the anxiety that may be engendered, nor is it discouraged since this behavior may be necessary to resolve the child's difficulties. Regression should be allowed to occur as a natural phenomenon.

Unless a child is psychotic, the regression is limited in time or to specific areas of difficulty and it may seem almost paradoxical in that the child is functioning at more advanced levels of development in other areas. For example, an 8-year-old boy may drink from the baby bottle, but at the same time maintain his scholastic level and ability to compete with his peers socially.

THE PLAYROOM

Child therapy should take place in a room designed to meet the needs of the child. Unfortunately, most therapists do not use a playroom for their sessions with children. An office puts an undue burden on children as the emphasis in an office is on talking. Further, the need to be careful about messes may inhibit a child from expressing issues because the necessary spontaneity is constrained by an office for adults.

The playroom should be between 110 and 120 square feet, to give the child room to move about and play, with washable walls and floors. A sink with hot and cold running water, for play and cleanup, is also important. Good lighting, heating, and ventilation are other necessities. A table and two chairs, a wastebasket for trash, shelves, and a cabinet for storage complete the bare necessities.

TOYS

Children use a variety of toys and materials to express themselves. However, some materials have been found to be more productive than others. The toys should include two anatomically correct dolls, one male and one female, that wet, blankets, diapers, baby clothing, bed and bottle, a simple dollhouse, furniture, toy family members, Velcro dart board, a sturdy punching bag and gloves, Tinker Toys and Legos, easel, paint, brushes and paper, hand puppets, board games (Battleship, Checkers, Sorry, Yahtzee, Triominoes), a small sandbox and sand toys, wet and reusable modeling clay, puzzles, books (the two I have found most helpful are *Where Did I Come From?* by Peter Mayle [1973] and *The Secret Worry* by Elissa Benedek [1984]), two nursing bottles, tabletop blocks, paper and pencils, crayons, paste, Scotch tape, scissors and ruler, and playing cards. In addition, each child should have her or his own box of toys that no other child has access to. This set of toys should be geared to the special needs of the child, and could include cap gun and caps, toy soldiers, small racing cars (I like using a police car, which may represent controls, and a fire truck, which may represent help and/or therapy), small dolls, drawing paper and crayons, and so on.

These play materials have been found to help children express both conscious and unconscious conflicts effectively. While each child uses play material in his own way, there are some common, symbolic meanings associated with the items in the playroom.

Amorphous materials, including water, paint, and clay, are provided as part of the basic material in the playroom because they lend themselves to multiple and contrasting uses, constructive and destructive play, and soothing. Water play is often helpful for enuretic and aggressive children, whose early need for satisfaction and soothing was not met or had to be given up too quickly. The children's feelings can be worked on by seemingly aimless pouring of water from one receptacle to another. Sometimes water is mixed with clay or paint to make a magic potion. Children may use water in a compensatory way. An example of this is a boy who was expelled from school because of urinating against the building. While at the clinic he offered to get tap water for the therapist to water her plants.

Clay is one of the most satisfactory amorphous materials since it can serve so many purposes. It can be fashioned into food, feces, and rolled into snakes. Aggression can be expressed by making bombs of clay, and when shaped into teachers, parents, or siblings, annihilation can follow readily. Part of its value lies in the tactile satisfaction it affords. Finger paint also gives tactile satisfactions and can profitably be used by the constricted child. At first many children find finger painting distasteful or too anxiety producing. They may want to use a paint brush or only the tips of their fingers, or may need another type of play materials as an introduction. Eventually they may become interested in messing and should not be expected to produce pictures. Finger painting is possibly the best material for the nonverbal child. Unconscious conflicts are often resolved by repetition, without verbalization by the child or interpretation by the therapist.

Four-year-old Jane walked out of the playroom with brown finger paint over the front of her legs while her face and arms were covered with green paint. She announced to her mother, "I'm a tree!" Mother's response, interestingly, was, "I'm so glad she can finally relax."

Water paint, crayons, drawing materials, and chalk and chalk-board are other examples of amorphous material. These materials are more structured and less expressive than finger paint, water, or clay, but are useful to children who find more suggestive material such as clay or finger paints too threatening. Often children's draw-ings and paints reveal diagnostic impressions. A house without doors or windows may confirm an impression of withdrawal. Colors used are often significant. Progress in treatment can sometimes be mea-sured by transition from the use of black and brown to the use of brighter colors. A child may portray a violent fight between two men-of-war, filling the drawing with planes and bombs. The chalk and chalkboard may be used similarly, but they commonly carry associations with school and learning problems.

The dollhouse and doll family are often used to portray the conflicts in children's homes and their relationships with parents and siblings. Daily routines, sleeping arrangements, and deprivations are revealed, too. Sometimes children may feel comfortable enough to share family problems as early as the first interview through the use of the innocuous dollhouse and doll family. Although children may communicate feelings about early experiences through the use of the dollhouse, they usually relive their experiences with parents and other adults in their current life. Nursing and wetting dolls may be fed and cared for as tenderly as the child would like to be treated. Maltreatment of the dolls may show feelings toward a sibling or represent the child's treatment by the parents.

Most children are afraid to reveal the anger and hostility they feel because of fear of retaliation and/or loss of love. The punching bag is one way in which children can learn to express these feel-ings. It can represent a peer, sibling, teacher, the therapist, or the parents. Children may also express self-hatred by letting the bag rebound on themselves. Feeling about the self may be apparent in remarks about their inability to hit the target with the dart gun. They may also use the gun to express anger and rage, gleefully shooting the entire doll family.

Building blocks also have multiple uses: creative construction, hostile destruction, and in combination with material such as guns they can become forts or bombs. Tinker toys can be used similarly. Toy soldiers stimulate expression of hostility, and children often use them in conjunction with the building blocks. Cars are used to express aggression and fantasies of omnipotence. Hand puppets are used like a telephone to communicate with the therapist, or they can be used like the doll family to indirectly express a wide range of feelings.

Dolls are used by the child who is sexually curious or has other identity problems, since children find sex problems difficult to verbalize. They are also used to recapitulate their own experiences of being parented, or to express wishes for particular kinds of handling by parents.

Models are useful for children who have poor motivation for schoolwork, who lack self-confidence, who are poorly organized psychologically, or who need to have the success of achievement. These models should be carefully chosen because a child will only be more frustrated if the model is too difficult and causes repeated failure. Thus, one might begin with snap-together models, progress through simple models with relatively few parts that can be completed in one session, to larger, more complex models taking several sessions to build and requiring attention to detail, the ability to follow instructions, and fine motor coordination.

On psychological testing, 8-year-old Gene was found to be poorly organized psychologically. He felt he could do whatever he wanted, which presented problems for his teacher as he repeatedly threw temper tantrums when faced with a task he did not want to tackle. In the playroom he played with his back to me for quite a while, softly talking through his play. In one session he settled upon a complex wooden model. His initiation of the task replicated his poor internal organization. I intervened, suggesting we do the model one step at a time, beginning with reading the directions. He impulsively lunged for pieces without having given the instruction sheet an adequate perusal. He was unable to match a piece with its drawing and often made errors as he created the model. We made many models with my providing the structure and Gene functioning well within the confines. Slowly he took over the structure and model building. His behavior in school gradually improved and he talked about his successes in the classroom.

The foregoing description of the uses of basic material by children is not exhaustive. Children can project their conflicts and fantasies onto any kind of material. It is essential that the therapist observe carefully what the child is doing and develop sensitivity to the child's feelings, as it is the understood experience that generates change.

4

DEVELOPMENTAL
PLAY THEMES:
THE PRESCHOOL YEARS

While play is the medium of communication in child therapy, this does not mean that children do not communicate verbally. Rather, play and play behaviors are the more complete statements of the child's concerns. The younger the child, the more important it is for the child to externalize thoughts and ideas so as to know and understand what is being thought and felt. As children are limited in their ability either to verbally explain their feeling states or to give clear statements of their concerns, it is our task to understand the play behavior of the child. Familiarity with child development can aid us in placing the child's expressed concern within the appropriate developmental context at two levels. One level addresses the developmental age of the problem behaviors and the other considers the child's range and level of functioning. In this way interventions can be more appropriately and effectively developed. This chapter presents a brief overview of development.

BIRTH TO EIGHTEEN MONTHS

Psychological theories of emotional and cognitive development between birth and 18 months use a variety of terms: the oral stage (Freud 1905), the stage of trust vs. mistrust (Erikson 1950), the sensory-motor stage (Piaget 1952), and the stage of separation-individuation (Mahler 1968). Each of these theoreticians has contributed to our understanding of the development of children. While I will refer to each of these theories, my primary emphasis will be on current understandings of infancy as developed through research. This research has demonstrated that from birth the infant is responsive to and seeks human interaction. The infant is not a passive recipient of ministration but is an active participant in the interpersonal interaction.

A relationship between mother and infant develops based on a mutual dialogue (Lichtenberg 1983, Stern 1973). This dialogue is the prototype of conversational turn taking. The baby coos, the mother responds in kind, the baby then makes more conversational sounds, the mother responds again, and so on. The general caregiving activities of the mother and playful and conversational interactions between mother and infant provide the foundation for attachment as well as the development of boundaries and separateness in the relationship. Lichtenberg (1983) suggests that in this crucial, highly synchronized dance between baby and mother, the infant controls the amount of stimulation he receives by turning away from the source of the stimulation when it is too intense to handle and returning when he has comforted himself. The infant also signals the mother for initiation of the dialogue by reproducing those behaviors that have engaged the mother in the past. This further underscores the competence of the infant and the active role of the baby in the relationship with mother.

The infant's sense of well-being is contingent upon the extent to which he can confidently expect and trust the mother to respond to and satisfy his needs. In addition, the mother's reactions, feelings, attitudes, and beliefs are transmitted to the infant through the caregiving process and the ways in which the mother responds to the infant in general.

> A woman I had been seeing for psychotherapy brought her 3-month-old son to a session so that I could see the child. During the course of the session he began fussing and she breast-fed him while continuing to talk with me. The child nursed for a short time then stopped. He began cooing and looking at her very attentively. The impression I gained was of her being called by the child to pay attention to him. When she attended to the child he began to nurse contentedly. When she resumed talking to me, the child once again stopped nursing, calling to her. He seemed to desire an interaction with his mother and could initiate familiar interactive patterns with her.

No one needs to teach children to become autonomous. Early developmental growth pushes the infant to deal with his increasing physical abilities through repetition, which leads to competence. However, it is only when the infant is adequately attached that it can respond to the beckoning of the larger environment and begin to explore beyond the orbit of the mothering relationship. By 6 to 8 months of age, the infant is more alert and has an increasing repertoire of motor skills. Investment in practicing the developing motor skills directs the child's attention away from mother and toward the environment. This can be noted in the new and distinct look of alertness, persistence, and goal directedness in infants from the time they are 6 month of age.

The child now studies people's faces to a much greater extent than previously. The child seems to compare new images with those of known caregiving adults. The apprehension and anxiety that the child expresses at this time does not reflect an actual fear of strangers, but rather an inability to fully comprehend the similarities and differences between known and unknown faces. Typically the interested adult intrudes into the space of the child, which results in the baby's discomfort. When babies are given a chance to move toward a stranger at their own pace, typical stranger anxiety reactions do not occur.

Regardless of the apprehension of leaving mother, the pull of the environment beckons the child to reach out and explore. The fear of exploration is made bearable by a mother who is not only predictable and reliable but who also supports and encourages exploration, and is there to return to. A mother who can't be trusted to be there upon return cannot be left (Furman 1982).

There are several activities that are characteristic of this period. When the child starts creeping, he does not initially go far because the advantages of roaming are outweighed by the uncertainties of too much distance from the mother. Creeping is therefore oriented around the mother. The child regularly checks back to confirm that the security of home base still exists in spite of the reaching out and creeping away. This checking back, or refueling, varies in form depending on the particular needs of the child and the nature of the relationship with the caregiver.

The characteristic patterns of creeping away and checking back/refueling are the bases for a number of games the child begins to play during this period of development. These games are experiments with the meaning of separateness and object permanence.

> *Peek-a-boo*: The earliest rendition is played at about 5 months of age. The caregiver's face disappears behind her hands and the baby experiences the tension of being alone. When the caregiver's face reappears the baby relaxes and coos and smiles, which is also mirrored on the caregiver's face.
>
> *Catch me*: The baby creeps off and checks back to determine if he is being pursued. The baby wants to be pursued and be caught and also to escape. A typical resolution to these mutually exclusive desires is for the caregiver to pursue until the baby turns and seeks contact.

Tossing away: By about 10 months the baby will frequently toss away something that he has been given, such as a spoon, food, or toy, and waits/expects the item to be returned. This activity explores and tests that there is a willing retrieving partner, and that what goes away can come back.

These games enable the baby to explore and master separations as well as develop understanding regarding the permanence of objects. In this period children make some tentative moves toward the outside world, which entices them. To do this they must have security and confidence in the caregiver. To the extent that certainty in the availability of mother is missing, children will experience difficulties.

Over the course of this period children develop from crawling and paddling to free and upright locomotion. This, combined with continued development, provides them with a much wider exposure to the world and their active roles in it.

For several months children practice and perfect the skills they have already accomplished. They become absorbed with exploration. The child's absorption in these activities does not exclude the caregiver, although at times it appears so. However, the child's need for refueling is still apparent and strong. As before, the form of the refueling varies. Some children must touch their caregiver, others need only to see or hear her from a distance.

Falls, bangs, and bruises do not matter much because now the child is the "doer," not the "done-to." The most striking feature of this period is the child's elation, which arises from the pleasure inherent in the exercise of new skills. In contrast to the elation, there also occurs "low-keyedness" (seriousness and pensiveness). Although children seem oblivious to their caregiver's presence, when she's away it becomes apparent that her presence is still essential. As Kaplan (1978) stated, the child "lowers sails until she returns" (p. 177). (This is why babysitters will report that children of this age have been

wonderfully quiet and well behaved while the mother was away.)
The baby's mood is down as he focuses inward in an apparent attempt to conjure up an image of the mother to comfort and soothe
himself in the absence of the parent(s).

Also noted in this period is the appearance of the "security
blanket." The blanket seems to symbolizes the comforting of the
caregiver, a skill the child is beginning to develop for himself. The
child, in using the blanket for comforting, has begun to develop
those skills that are necessary for him to comfort himself and modu-
late his needs and drives. According to Tolpin (1971), "When the
infant begins to use his blanket to soothe himself, he has created
something—that is, he had endowed an inconsequential bit of the
'external world' with a capacity to restore or improve his inner
equilibrium. . . . He has at hand a means to calm himself" (p. 321).

At about 15 to 18 months the momentum of growth slows.
By this time the child's mind has developed enough so that he begins
to create symbols, concepts, and images. Symbols and words allow
the child to conceptualize an object without actually having it in
sight. The child can manipulate images so that now, anything can
be anything else. The child can carry his caregivers around with
him as an image (as well as a blanket), relinquishing the necessity
for the actual person, and reinforcing the knowledge that objects
and people can exist even when not seen.

Play themes from this first year and a half of development as
seen in later childhood revolve around:

> feeding and being fed,
> being taken care of and caring for others,
> swallowing and devouring,
> being devoured and biting,
> being bitten,
> losing and finding,
> hiding and finding,
> dropping and retrieving,

sleeping and being awake,
losing important people,
being abandoned,
being left alone,
fearing death and/or annihilation,
being satisfied and being deprived,
getting one's share and not getting one's share,
sharing and not sharing,
being separate from others and being one with others.

The ability to make-believe or pretend to enact the themes just mentioned requires the use of symbolic thinking. This ability begins during this sensorimotor period and is connected to the use of language. At this early level, play themes are usually centered around everyday activities.

The relationship between the therapist and a child who is expressing difficulties from this level of development may reflect or emphasize the child's sense of satisfaction or feelings of deprivation, of separateness from or unification with the therapist. Defensive maneuvers of the child include the most primitive defenses such as denial, introjection, splitting, and projection.

> Ten-year-old Gary, during one of the beginning therapy sessions, asked me if I had a nickname. After I responded in the negative he asked if he could give me one. Gary decided to call me "Harry." When I asked him how he came to choose Harry as a nickname for me he explained that his name and my nickname went together; they rhymed.

This interaction is reflective of the severe separation–individuation problem of this child stemming from difficulties in dealing with developmental imperatives inherent in the first year and a half of life as described above. Gary's name and my name had to be quite close, which seemed to provide him with a seamless connection to me.

EIGHTEEN MONTHS TO THREE YEARS

The period from 18 months to 3 years has been known as the anal stage, the stage of autonomy vs. shame and doubt, and the preoperational phase. The main theme is one of holding on and letting go. Tasks critical for development include:

1. Learning of independence
2. Development of inner controls
3. Imitation
4. Development of peer interactions
5. Clarification of the self and self-concept
6. Increased verbal expression for communication.

In the previous period children's activities in mastering and perfecting their skills moved them away from their caregivers. Now the world, its objects, and children's discoveries are only meaningful when shared with another, important person. This is frequently demonstrated in a continuous activity of bringing things to this person to show and share, and after a while taking them back and placing them where they had been, only to start the process again. The mastery of new words and the expanding vocabulary provide a new power to command and ask for things. With the acquisition of language, the child can develop symbolic play to help cope with being helpless and alone (Winnicott 1958). Through play the child assures himself that aloneness can be managed when he takes the part of the caregiver. For example, a child may cuddle a doll and reassure it that mother/father/caregiver will only be gone a little while and is certain to return. The child is actually reassuring himself. Nevertheless, the caregiver is at once wanted and not wanted. As greater separateness occurs, so do the child's confusion and ambivalence. The drama of increasing separation and individuation is played out in physical space by repeated sequences of getting closer and moving away, which are not only a reflection of the child's ambivalent feelings but also a demonstration of the struggle to solve the problem of a comfortable distance in the relationship. This is a behavioral enactment of the struggle around closeness and distance that is taking place in the child's mind. The conflict is enacted via the following characteristic activities:

> *Clinging/pushing away*: When the caregiver tries to leave, the child will cling to and protest until there is an attempt to embrace and console the child, at which point the caregiver is pushed away and the child is angered by the comforting attempt.
>
> *Darting away*: Noting that the caregiver is preoccupied with some activity, the child zooms past and away recklessly, with the apparent expectation that he will be swooped up. However, when this occurs the child often vigorously resists with giggling and squirming.
>
> *Shadowing*: The child attempts to undo the separateness by sticking close to—but not touching—the caregiver. The distance is held constant, helping the child to resolve the issue of closeness–separation.
>
> *Saying no*: This is a means of overcoming feelings of helplessness with an assertion of autonomy. It also provides a vehicle for some expression of anger. As a prelude to saying yes, it also helps the child define a comfortable emotional distance.

To always win or always lose these no-saying battles can create great difficulties for the child. Should the child always win, in later life he may feel vulnerable and powerless when he can't control someone else (this is the "spoiled brat" syndrome). To always lose fosters feelings of vulnerability and powerlessness in the child from the start. When an adequate balance is struck between these extremes the child is helped to integrate opposites.

During this period of development temper tantrums make their appearance. They are an attempt to deal with the growing sense of individuation the child has begun to develop and his struggles with distance and closeness in the relationship with the caregiver. The appropriate parental response is empathic, allowing the child to discover that the world can't be destroyed by aggression. The child is usually relieved to find that the world is okay when the tantrum ends, and it is not uncommon for the child to then seek consolation.

Fathers, if they are not the primary caregivers, play an important role in the separation-individuation process for both boys and girls. They are a familiar other-than-mother figure, and therefore a source of solace as well as excitement. These qualities of solace and excitement that children seek from their fathers come at the height of the separation-individuation struggle, which is played out primarily with the mother. Mahler (1968) labeled this period as rapprochement and described the behaviors of the toddler as attempting to reduce his sense of omnipotence and vulnerability. The toddler also attempts to define himself in relation to others through these behaviors.

For Mahler, the ability to accomplish the tasks of this period is contingent on what happened in earlier periods. In the crisis of rapprochement the parents must be empathic to the ambivalence of the child and be emotionally available to him. How the child is able to cope with the letdown of the rapprochement crisis can have an impact on the manner in which the inevitable letdowns of later life are managed.

These first three years are known as the preoedipal years. In general, preoedipal play revolves around the all-important relationship to the mothering figure. Other people are secondary or used instrumentally to accomplish various aims. An additional theme is that of being left and abandoned. In general, the passive experiences of these first years are dealt with by a reversal of roles, by turning the passive experience into an active one.

Children express their awareness of their smallness and vulnerability in their play, which has a repetitiveness and rigidity. This is seen as an outgrowth of the reversal of passive into active and an attempt to create a safe world for themselves, rather than experiencing this safety as arising from the activities of the parents.

The major play themes of this period of development include:

being hurt, scolding, and being angry;
destroying, hurting, punishing, and being punished;
being witch, devil, and monster;
being controlled and controlling;
messing, dirtying, cleaning, and order.

The therapeutic relationship has qualities of conformity or negativism and resistance. Rapprochement issues of moving away and coming close are directly played out in the course of the session. Defenses from this level of development could include those from the earlier period as well as reaction formation, undoing, displacement-reversal, aggression against the self, imitation, and beginning identification.

THREE YEARS TO SIX YEARS

In this period children develop a stable sense of self and an identity. They also develop mental representations of themselves as separate and distinct from those of important others. The bulk of the development of a stable sense of self is accomplished by establishing an emotional object constancy. This in turn allows children to function independently in spite of the inevitable tension, discomfort, and frustration experienced in daily functioning. With object constancy the mother or caregiver can be remembered in periods of absence, which allows children to tolerate separations. Children can carry those important aspects of the mother around with them until they can integrate those important aspects into their own personality structure.

Like the tasks of the previous phases, consolidation is not a complete and discrete occurrence. It is a gradual process with periods of progression interspersed with regression. For optimal consolidation and further development, there must have been the experience of trust and confidence through regular and reliable response by the mother in previous periods.

Three Years

The basic developmental tasks children sought to master during the first three years are now weathered. Three-year-olds are free to use abilities and skills to find out who they are and what they can do. Throughout the next two to three years, which constitutes the time span of this stage of emotional development, adults, and parents in particular, remain important figures, as it is from parents that children establish and bask in the glow of reflected competence and power.

The child's energies are primarily directed toward establishing a self-identity and a greater understanding of reality. While there are more observable controls and understanding of differences between people and objects, the personality structure of the child is not firmly set. The resulting flexibility allows for the continuing growth and development of the personality.

These years are years of great growth in knowledge and independence. There is also tremendous growth within the child as well. The child is beginning to form basic attitudes about himself, the people around him, and the world he lives in. The attitudes that develop about the self and others will color behavior throughout development. Within this context, the child is slowly moving away from self-centeredness. He is beginning to learn to share with others and to understand the rights of others. He is better able now to embed himself in a time sequence of yesterday, today, and tomorrow. Relationships, such as mother–father, male–female, and son–daughter, are learned, as are the differences between wishes and reality. The child learns what it is to be a girl or boy.

In all of the tasks that the child comes to grips with during these years, play and fantasy serve as the primary medium for working out not only developmental tasks but also the various crises of growing up. It is through play that the child learns to bring frightening things down to size so that they may be coped with.

While the child is now challenged by his environment to be active and master new tasks, the 3-year-old is in transition from the previous stage of development. The child's compliance helps establish the close relationship with the significant people in the environment that will allow him to try out the roles he views.

The charm and equilibrium of the 3-year-old are replaced by the oppositional and refusing 3½-year-old, who insists upon things being done his way. This second half of the year is one of turbulence. The child asserts himself in direct opposition to the caregiver specifically. While 3½-year-olds are quite resistant to demands, they are not averse to making demands on other people in the environment. At the same time the child exhibits more fearfulness and hesitancy in many areas of functioning. Fine-motor tremors can be present so that building with blocks seems to be more clumsily performed than previously; stuttering in speech is also not uncommon. The child may speak in a whiny, demanding tone of voice, which indicates some real distress. Vision seems to pose some difficulties, and it is not uncommon for the 3½-year-old to complain of not being able to see well, which is clearly demonstrated by holding books and other objects close to the eyes.

The tensions these behaviors bespeak appear to increase to the point where the child seems to fall to pieces. Nevertheless this confused and confusing child is often sensitive and intuitive to the feelings of others. Having resolved the developmental tasks of the previous three years the child now struggles with being like an important figure in his life.

Identification

Identification is a long process that involves producing in oneself the behavior of the model chosen. According to White (1959), the models used signify for the child the prototypes of competence the child wishes to reproduce within himself. Identification, however, is a slowly evolving process that begins with the reproduction of those acts of behavior that the child can already perform. The process is an active one of changing one's established behavior to make it more like the model. However, identification is not a simple act of copying, but rather a very powerful form of learning that involves perception of the model, choice of specific behaviors, and an interpretation/reproduction of them in behavior. The behaviors become selectively molded into masculine and feminine roles through the differential responses of adults to the exhibited behaviors. The responses of the adult have an important influence on the choice of objects for identification. They serve to define for boys and girls the kinds of competencies that are most appropriate for them.

To admire another person and want to be like that person is not only a compliment from the child but also implies that the child has developed some sense of a unified self and can take the role of the "other." Further, the child seems to have reached a point of understanding whereby he can contemplate his place in the family and his relationship to other people in general. While still quite egocentric, the child nevertheless can move outside himself for short periods of time, and thereby compare himself with adults.

Ideally, children grow up in an environment that includes a mother and a father. Attachment to both parents must occur for the child to develop adequately. Physical care of the infant results in sensual stimulation of the child; this occurs with both parents when they are engaged in the care of the infant. While only the mother can breast-feed a child, the child soon eats other food, which both parents can provide. However, in most families in Western society, mothers provide most of the care since they spend more time with the child than does the father. However, this does not exclude him from the child-rearing process.

By the time a child is 3, he can label his sex and draw a parallel between himself and the parent of the same sex. When the child can do this with some degree of certainty, imitation of the role model presented by each of the parents can be tried out. The little girl does things with and just like her mother, but with her father as well. The little boy does things with and just like his father, but with his mother as well.

Once the child has tried on the various behaviors designated for his or her particular gender, the child can then move into identification proper and try out a coherent behavior pattern. In other words, the child can employ the attitudes of the role in interaction with significant others. The little girl begins to respond to her father much as she has observed her mother respond to him, and his responses to her are similar to his responses to his wife. The little boy responds to his mother much in the same way he has observed his father respond to her, and she in turn responds to him in ways similar to her responses to her husband. This oedipal situation or love affair between the child and the parent of the opposite sex is an exploration of behaviors and roles the child has observed in his relationships with important adults in the environment. Complicating the identification process is the level of the child's cognitive development. As Piaget (1952) discussed, children cannot entertain the possibility that you can be two things at the same time. For instance, the child cannot grasp the idea that his mother or father is his grandmother's child. Being his parent means that the parent cannot also be a child. It will take some more cognitive growth to begin to piece this problem together appropriately. In the meantime children explain that they will become either the mother or father while the mother or father becomes the child. Names will also be exchanged and thus the children can "marry" their opposite-sexed parent. As parents deal with the impossibility of the child marrying the parent, children slowly and reluctantly give up the hope of being the parental spouse. However, this takes time but also needs further development in cognitive functioning to accomplish.

It is neither castration anxiety nor penis envy that propels the child toward the resolution of the oedipal situation, but rather the clear disengagement of the parents from their part in the oedipal triangle as well as cognitive development. As the oedipal situation resolves itself, children of both sexes express a great deal of anger toward the parent of the opposite sex arising out of the felt rejection.

With identification, conscience becomes established in a way it has not been previously, and with the development of a conscience, guilt is more in evidence. Guilt is one of the avenues by which the controls necessary for adequate social functioning become internal to the child, who previously had controls imposed upon him. Guilt feelings serve as a warning signal for the child who has internal controls, when an impulse to engage in a "naughty" act comes over him. When the child can produce his own warning signals, independent of the actual presence of the adult, he is on the way to developing a conscience. This raises the question as to why a child should do the right thing. The close ties between feelings of being loved and approved of by parents and feelings of self-esteem combine to produce feelings of self-acceptance. A fall in the esteem of the parents produces a drop in self-esteem, which in turn leads to feelings of guilt. The experience of guilt for wrongdoing is necessary for the development of self-control.

Identification and the concomitant development of a conscience is a long, slow process. The 3½-year-old still vacillates between imitation and identification. The 4-year-old, on the other hand, is more firmly entrenched in the process of identification. However, identification does not cease with the establishment of a sense of self; it is a lifelong process.

The preschooler identifies primarily with parents and views them as strong and idealized heroes and heroines. The school-age child identifies with more glamorous and prestigious figures outside the family. The 8-year-old boy or girl may swagger like a general or concoct chemical compounds like a scientist. The 10-year-old models himself after heroines and heroes that appear stronger, more daring, more intriguing than Mom and Dad.

Typically boys are expected to be strong, courageous, assertive, and ambitious. Girls are expected to be sociable, well mannered, and neat, and to be afraid of threatening objects and to withdraw from unusually difficult problem situations. Not only are the sexes trained differently for social role behavior, but social classes train differently.

Both boys and girls of the lower class become aware of their sex-role patterns sooner than middle-class children. The lower-class boys reach a stable, high level of sex identification by the time they are 5, while middle-class boys do not do so until 6 or beyond. At the age of 6, lower-class girls make definite sex-appropriate choices, but middle-class girls do not show clear-cut acceptance of their role even by the age of 8.

The peer group for the preschool, the school-age child, and the adolescent provides an opportunity to learn how to interact with peers, how to deal with hostility and dominance, how to relate to a leader, and how to lead others. Through discussions with peers the child may learn that others share similar problems, conflicts, and complex feelings, which is reassuring. This discovery that other boys and girls also become angry with their fathers and mothers relieves tension and guilt.

Four Years

The 4-year-old's behavior, in being out of bounds, in focusing on the development of physical/motor skills, in being intrusive, and in seeming unawareness of his impact on others in the environment, is reminiscent of the 1½-year-old. However, the child of this era is more agile and coordinated. The use of large muscles provides the child with a great sense of pleasure and accomplishment. While the body is hard at work so is the mind and tongues of these assertive, boastful children. They are demanding of attention, asking how and why; they question, listen for an answer, question again, and so forth until the subject is more than exhausted. More often than not, the 4-year-old wants an audience, which provides the child with a sense of being in a relationship. The questioning seems to be a means for testing out whether or not the child is competent and can have an impact upon an adult.

Four-year-olds tend to be quite imaginative and changeable, so that as they begin to make a drawing of one object, they wind up completing something that is different from their original intention. Their imaginativeness also leads to some wild fabrications. One 4-year-old girl came home from nursery school announcing that a tornado was a big turtle, and nothing but time could dissuade her of her belief. Another youngster of 4, when asked if he would like to come to Sunday school as he was getting to be a big enough boy, said that he wanted to because he was now 4 and then quickly stated that he was 6 years old. When asked if that meant he was going into first grade he calmly took the question in stride and told his questioner that he was.

Four-year-olds play with words and numbers, exaggerating amounts and making two syllable words out of one. The 4-year-old, in general, is out of bounds, intruding into adults' ways of doing things, into their bodies and into their ears with their loud insistent voices. The 4-year-old often steps on the toes of the important adults in the environment, and can often be in interpersonal difficulty. They are also quite embarrassing to the adult, for what is on their minds is on their tongues, and hence family secrets are told at the least opportune moment. Perceptions that adults have learned to leave unsaid are often shared out loud by 4-year-olds.

Five Years

In contrast with the 4-year-old, who is experimenting with his world and is out of bounds a good deal of the time, the 5-year-old is very much close to home. Five is quite conforming, and looks for the praise that comes with that conformity. Five is a talker, and humor becomes a part of the child's repertoire. The turbulence of this stage of development calms during this year. The child has resolved some of the developmental tasks, and is now consolidating gains in preparation for the final phase of childhood.

During ages 3 to 6 years new developmental urges propel the child to master increasingly complex developmental tasks. These years are known as the phallic, initiative vs. guilt, and intuitive thought stage. The developmental tasks children must deal with include:

1. beginning of same sex identification
2. development of a conscience
3. finding a place with family and peers
4. development of increasing self-responsibility
5. beginning to ask and answer the question, "Who Am I?"

Behaviorally, 3- to 4½-year-olds exhibit a great deal of interest in genitalia and nudity. They are struggling with the meaning of the differences between the sexes. This curiosity is also expressed in other aspects of their functioning. They take things apart for investigation and as a way of teaching themselves about how things function. Children are competitive, challenging, braggarts, boasters, exhibitionistic, attention seeking, assertive, and forceful. They may also exhibit phobias and fears revolving around bodily damage. The play behavior typically revolves around stereotyped sex-role play, buffoonery and clowning, shyness and modesty, and exaggerated masculinity or femininity.

Oedipal play productions are fluid and have endless change. There are a great variety of plots, themes, rules, and emotions. The children exhibit a blindness to age differences, often acting as parental partners. They telescope time and attempt to establish the future now. Specific play themes include:

interest in genitals and touching;
fear of genitals and touching;
taking things apart to see what is inside;

avoidance of looking inside of things;
concerns about being extraordinary or worthless, being admired
    or ridiculed, being strong or weak;
body integrity or disintegration.

For girls:

sex-stereotyped play (e.g., mothering, home-making, ballerina,
    nurse, teacher);
concerns about being a girl;
worth or worthlessness as a girl.

For boys:

sex-stereotyped play (e.g., shooting, stabbing, warring, police-
    man, fireman, milkman);
concerns about being a boy;
worth or worthlessness as a boy.

Children engage in complex family and sociodramatic play,
with each child playing the role of the same-sex parent. The children talk about marriage and wanting to be a parent. In conjunction with this they begin asking sexual questions, show interest in
learning, explaining, achieving, mastering difficulties, solving problems, and social activities. They are also seductive, manipulative,
friendly, cooperative, charming, flirtatious, coy, and competitive
with people of the same sex.

Specific play themes include family play, playing the same-sex
parent or the opposite-sex parent, marriage, sexuality, exploring,
learning, social activities, complex dramatic play and small group
games, and play at achieving, mastery, and solving problems. For
girls there are additional concerns about being like or different from
mother, competition with mother for father, with father for mother,
with siblings for each parent, and concerns about succeeding or
failing in competition.

For boys there are additional concerns about being like or different from father, competition with father for mother and mother for father, and concern about succeeding or failing in competition.

Issues in the therapeutic relationship may center around competition, guilt, body damage and integrity, activity and passivity, competence and incompetence, confidence and insecurity. Defenses seen may include all the earlier ones mentioned as well as the more current ones of isolation, intellectualization, regression, and repression.

5

DEVELOPMENTAL PLAY THEMES: THE SCHOOL YEARS

The school years have been known as the latency age, the stage of industry vs. inferiority, and the stage of concrete operations, all with a basic theme of competence. There are no major developmental tasks. However, the main concerns of children revolve around the establishment of competence in all areas of functioning. During this stage children learn constructive productions, carrying tasks through to completion, and the meaningful exercise of skills. The play of children during these years does not have the clarity seen in the younger child. There is much social interplay in games, with each child functioning within a role, with supporting co-players. Attachments to peers also gain in importance. However, children are more critical of themselves and may feel uneasy and unhappy over their achievements. This makes them feel vulnerable. Along with the increased vulnerability is an evoked wishful fantasy of "I can go back and start all over again." Games with rules provide children with the possibility of starting again and again, with each attempt having a different ending. Games also channel sexual and aggressive drives, which children must learn to monitor and master without the aid of parental control.

Children from 6 to 12 are usually resistant to unstructured play activity and are seldom interested in examining dreams, fantasy life, or intimate relationships with others. They fear being thrown back to more immature feelings and undermining their newly won maturity. Attempts to discuss problems to relieve their fear and apprehension cause embarrassment, while the need for control increases the tendency for youngsters to withhold.

While the first 6 years of a child's life can be broken down into clearly defined stages, the years from 6 to 12 cannot. But there are two distinct phases of development. The years from 6 to 9 seem to have a coherence of their own. At 9 the formal period of childhood ends. The years from 9 to 12 seem to be another coherent period, a no-man's-land between childhood and adolescence. However, this does not mean that within each of these ages children are alike. The 6-year-old is as different from the 7-year-old as the 7-year-old is from the 11-year-old.

SIX-YEAR-OLDS

The 6-year-old is thrust from the security of the home into the insecurity of five hours a day in the classroom. Whereas the child had the support and encouragement of family to help her over the rough spots of the day, the child must now depend upon herself to resolve conflicts. Furthermore, there are now limitations in a great many areas of functioning where there were few before. Compliance is now expected in areas that were formerly free-choice areas for the child. The child faces a new way of functioning and living. The changes and conflicts churn up not only the overt ways of functioning for children, but also the emotional life of the child.

Six-year-olds are self-centered and egocentric. They exhibit a great push to be first, best, "onliest," loved most. In the push to stand out above all others, they can be very stubborn and demanding of their own point of view, or at least of the supporter of the point of view they imagine powerful people hold. As a result, the teacher becomes the source of the most profound statements and is the ultimate authority in all instances. While this attitude stems from the child's limited understanding of the world, restricted cognitive functioning, and an inability to understand that different people have different skills to offer, there is the added factor that by placing the teacher above other important adults, the child can more easily make the needed break from home and parents in preparation for greater independence and individuation. As a means of fostering this further separation and differentiation, the child seems to become a tyrant, ordering people about and exhibiting an unusually strong stubborn streak, more effective than the stubbornness exhibited at age 2. The child is also sensitive and vulnerable to the pressures and underlying unspoken feelings present in the environment, although she may not always be able to respond to them as such.

Children at this age are active and seek out experiences. As a consequence, they run into much difficulty as they batter at the walls of the world they are trying to conquer. Emotional responses are expressed in extremes. If the child can batter the walls down, there are great expressions of joy; if the walls do not yield to bombardment, extremes of despair are much in evidence. In spite of the intensity of response to experiences exhibited by 6-year-olds, surprisingly they can be quite realistic, matter-of-fact, and down to earth. Perceptions have clarified and children are better able to assess their abilities as well as their limitations. Nevertheless, these characteristics of 6-year-olds make interpersonal relationships difficult, not only within the family but also among peers.

SEVEN-YEAR-OLDS

The dreaminess and withdrawn stance of the 7-year-old is the response to the impact of the struggles and battles that have occurred during the previous year. It is depressing to find that one is not always the first or the best, especially after one has struggled quite hard to establish this fact.

The child of 7 makes peace with the world, but is not at peace with herself. Children at this age seem to be sad and brooding, sometimes morbid, sometimes sulky, generally unhappy. The generalized sadness of the 7-year-old leads to a greater attachment to adults than was seen the previous year. This renewed closeness reflects the 7-year-old's awareness of her limitations and vulnerabilities.

For the 7-year-old, adults who seem to function without anyone telling them what to do have a magical quality. In fact, 7-year-olds are much into magic and magic tricks. Riddles are also an important part of their functioning, and they exhibit increased facility with language. The 7-year-old can carry on a lively conversation not only with adults but with peers as well.

Within this year, with the expressed and increasing concern of children as to what others think of them, we see the preparatory work for being 8. The first real conflicts begin at about this time revolving around the values and standards of home vs. the values and standards of peers. While children look for the support and approval of adults in the environment, the approbation of peers is becoming far more critical in propelling the child toward the establishment of competence.

EIGHT-YEAR-OLDS

The 8-year-old is far less moody and withdrawn than her 7-year-old counterpart. With greater competence one can see children becoming more evaluative of themselves, of interpersonal relationships, and of others. There is still a strong interest in adults, adult conversations, and adult behavior, but the child of this age is far more invested in the peer group than ever before. Feelings are still easily hurt, which leads to externalizing those feelings, as opposed to the 7-year-old who internalized feelings. As such the 8-year-old can be explosive, aggressive, egocentric, demanding, and tearful. With increased emphasis on right and wrong, the child begins to show some rather strong moral propensities and resents being talked down to and not treated with respect. Involvement in team games represents the child's continuing attempt and struggle to establish herself as a competent person, for example, being proficient in sports and being a worthwhile team member. Board games, now within the child's capabilities, become increasingly important to children as competence is tested: "Am I a winner or loser?" No matter the outcome, the game can be played again with a different result.

Boys and girls begin to segregate themselves, particularly at school (Thorne 1993). Acceptance by one's same-sex peer group puts the stamp of approval of competence on the child for behaving in a manner appropriate to the peer group's expectations.

During the year from 8 to 9 children seem to consolidate development:

1. There is a greater separation of the child from her family with increased reliance on the peer group for support and approval.
2. The child begins to establish her competence in many areas of functioning.
3. The child shows initiative in dealing with schoolwork on her own.
4. The child develops autonomy from parents and other adults.
5. The child trusts in her own abilities to cope with herself and the world.

PREADOLESCENCE (9–12)

Preadolescence, the years from 9 through 12 is a point in development that sees a divergence between boys and girls (Thorne 1993).

In general, children by this age have closed themselves off to adults, viewing them as a kind of "enemy." It is a time when the nicest children begin to behave in the "awfullest" manner (Redl and Wineman 1957), when the incidence of referrals to child guidance clinics are at its peak; and when children are really no longer children. But neither are they adolescents; rather, they exhibit the characteristics of both age groups.

Preadolescents are hard to live with because of their restlessness. Their hands seem to need constant occupation, they turn up the edges of books, they handle or manipulate any objects near to hand as well as their own bodies; they seem to be in perpetual motion. Infantile habits seem to crop up overnight for no apparent reason; funny gestures appear, facial tics begin, speech problems occur. In other areas these children express problems seen in younger children. On the other hand, the pressures of the developmental pushes toward adolescence result in sex becoming increasingly important. They diligently pursue information about sexual relationships, and the juicier and more graphic the information the better. They tend to be bored and uninterested in matter-of-fact explanations.

Girls consider themselves to be inferior to boys because they do not act like boys. Girls go through a period of wishing for the opportunities they see boys enjoying. The activity level and complex games that girls feel are open to boys but not to themselves contribute to a sense of not being happy with their femaleness.

> Eleven-year-old Beth came into treatment because she did not want to grow up, according to her mother. The youngster informed me she had decided she did not want to change her lifestyle. She told me she wanted to play football but that adults would not allow her to do so nor would the boys let her join them. She also said that her teacher did not like her because she did not wear dresses and she was not "prissy" like the other girls in class. She had no desire to be a boy but she did want to have the same freedom of activity that they had. A new girl in class who was also interested in playing football with her solved part of the issue of activity level.

Socially boys and girls give the impression they have no use for each other. This appearance is observable in the larger arena of school and playground. However, according to Thorne (1993) this aversion does not carry over in the more intimate areas of home and neighborhood, especially when same-sex peers are not available.

The fantasy life of children at this age is loaded with daydreams, which occupy a good deal of their time but which they cannot and do not communicate with others. They are easily offended and are constantly ready with accusations that the adult does not understand them and therefore they are being treated wrongly, and yet they are reckless and inconsiderate of the feelings of others. The daily life of children at this age becomes a chain of little irritations about little things; there are fights against the demands of obeying the rules, keeping appointed mealtimes, coming home, doing homework, going to bed at a prearranged hour, and keeping promises, especially with adults. With peers, however, preadolescents keep their commitments. Peers set the standards for acceptable behaviors to a greater degree than the parents. It is no wonder that adult–child relationships can be so disturbed at this period in a child's life. All the demands and regulations of living within a family are experienced as tyranny.

The organization of the child's personality is broken up or loosened, which allows for the modifications needed for the entrance into adolescence. During the breakup period, long forgotten or repressed impulses of earlier childhood arise for a while before they are discarded for good. This in part explains the return to infantile mannerisms. Standards and values lose their power and become ineffective; hence, the apparent lack of self-control that is often seen in these children. The conscience of the child also seems to lose its powers, which explains the child's apparent immunity to guilt feelings. Anxiety and conflict come to the surface, which is also why other mechanisms are in evidence, and why the group and clique become increasingly important, for it is the group and clique that not only lend support to the child who cannot be accepted by adults, but also set the standards for behavior that the adult once did.

There seems to be a coherent thread during the preadolescent years, which are the time of preparation for dealing with the tasks and problems of adolescence.

Nine-Year-Olds

Nine-year-olds tend to be so wrapped up in themselves and their own concerns that responsiveness to others, especially parents and other adults, is unimportant. They tend to be perfectionists, and when they do not meet their own standards they feel that something is wrong with them and especially with their bodies. As a result they express many hypochondriacal concerns. As Stolorow and Lachmann (1980) have suggested, when a person becomes hypochondriacal after ignoring their bodily selves, what we see is the beginning investment in the self. Nine-year-olds are at a point in development where they are beginning to be responsible for their bodies. But they are not sure they are capable of the task, so hypochondriasis is seen.

Nines with more intellectual and emotional maturity can be more critical of their productions, such as schoolwork, artistic creations, and game functioning, which is accompanied by whines and complaints of various kinds. With this supersensitivity to the various aspects of living, as well as the shift in focus of values and standards of behavior, the 9-year-old often looks very neurotic.

Ten-Year-Olds

While 10-year-olds continue to be hypochondriacal, they are in better balance with themselves and the world. Magic once again becomes an important feature in their lives, but in spite of their interest in the supernatural and all the spooky television programs, 10-year-olds are more matter-of-fact than they were the previous year. They seem more at ease with themselves, and are easier to live with and deal with. However, all the standards and routines of home may go by the wayside when the peer group is in need of them and the skills they can bring to activities.

Eleven-Year-Olds

Eleven-year-olds are quite verbal. Their speech productions, however, do not always have as their prime motivation communication with others. Rather their words have a stream-of-consciousness flavor. They talk for the sake of filling up a silence and possibly to listen to their ideas. They can be quarrelsome and argumentative, not only with their parents, but with other adults as well. While again critical of the adult world, they are also critical of themselves, to the extent that their self-esteem falls. This quality interferes with their ability to make decisions or to make clear and specific statements. They are couched in many qualifications. The breakup in personality structure seen at this age is reflective not only of the increasing pressure of the adolescent pushes and stress, but also of increasing intellectual development. The children are moving toward the final phase of the intellectual development as described by Piaget, the stage of formal operations.

DEVELOPMENTAL HAZARDS
OF THE SCHOOL-AGE CHILD

There is increasing energy to invest all possible efforts in producing. Opposing this is an ever-present pull toward a previous level of lesser production. The fear is supported by the fact that the child is still a child.

There is only one way of solving these fears of inferiority, by doing and mastering, by learning necessary skills. During these years the healthy child is frequently described as being "too big for his britches." The child devotes abundant energy to self-improvement and to conquest of people and things. The drive to succeed includes an awareness of the threat of failure, and this underlying fear impels the child to work harder to succeed. Children are very competitive at this age. Any halfway measure, any mediocrity will lead the child to a sense of inferiority—a feeling that must be combated in order to move on toward adulthood with self-assurance.

What determines whether a child suceeds or not? When a person becomes anxious, certain automatic defense processes beyond the level of awareness are triggered off. During this period two important defensive behaviors occur: withdrawal and retaliation in the face of anxiety. One can withdraw from anxiety-arousing situations, deny the threat, or avoid dealing with it, or one can attack the source of anxiety and attempt to conquer it. The tendency to flee or fight snowballs; every time the child runs, it becomes easier to do so the next time.

During preadolescence developmental tasks include:

1. crystallization of sex-role identification,
2. strengthening of the superego (conscience and values of society),
3. learning how to interact with peers,
4. development of academic skills.

The play themes focus on:

1. conquest of people and objects or being conquered by them,
2. competition interpersonally, with the consequence of being considered a winner or a loser.

Interpersonally, relationships are based on competence and incompetence, fighting or fleeing. Competition between people is a hallmark of these middle childhood years. In addition to all the defenses mentioned previously, regression and repression are the most common at this time.

6

INTERVENTION/ INTERPRETATION

While there are many ways to intervene in the resolution of difficulties in children, the recognition, acceptance, and understanding of the child's feelings are primary. There are many opinions about the role of interpretation in child therapy. At one extreme the Kleinians (Klein 1975, Winnicott 1977) make deep analytic statements to the child, while at the other extreme the client-centered therapists (Axline 1947) reflect feeling tones and do not interpret. Whatever the theoretical framework the therapist must have the flexibility to meet the child in the here and now and not from a fixed position. At a conference a child therapist told the audience he put children on the couch because they know why they were there and the couch encouraged children to free associate even when playing with the toys the therapists provided. Another therapist indicated that she took the child to a closet with toys, and allowed the child to choose one toy with which he played throughout the session. If the child wanted another toy the therapist would then interpret the child's request as resistance. Both of these therapists were aware that children express their feelings and concerns in play

with the use of toys. However, the child, with his needs was sub-
ordinated to the therapist's preconceptions of how children play and
should be treated irrespective of the needs of the child.

Therapists must respond to the uniqueness of each child with
flexibility and sensitivity. Thus a variety of interventions will be used
not only over time but also within any one individual session in
reaction to the verbal, behavioral and play communications of the
particular child.

> Gary, a 10-year-old boy, was sitting on the table, relaxing between
> innings in a baseball game we had been playing. I raised the issue
> of his punishment by his father—cleaning the bathroom for a
> week—because he had urinated in a paper bag and left it in his
> room. As I shared this information with him he blanched and tried
> to melt into the wall. Watching his terrified reaction I knew that
> any interpretation would not be useful to him and that reflecting
> on his feelings would not relax him. I felt that relief from the terror
> was most critical at that moment. I therefore decided upon a reality
> approach that would also express my acceptance of his behavior.
> I asked, "How did you keep it from leaking out of the bag?" The
> color came back into the child's face, his body relaxed, and he
> proceeded to tell me the rest of the story with some sense of
> pleasure. He had urinated not once, but twice into the bag and
> had put a lot of tissues in the bottom to "sop things up." Non-
> chalantly I suggested that it couldn't be much fun cleaning the
> bathroom for a whole week and that maybe he and I could talk
> about better ways of dealing with his angry feelings toward his
> father. The interpretation of Gary's feelings as anger was now easier
> for the child to accept.

My varied intervention levels, that is, helping the child to relax
enough to talk about the incident, dealing with the consequences
of his behavior, and linking the behavior with his feelings about his
father, helped Gary become aware of the consequences and reasons for his behavior.

Nine-year-old Mark asked questions perseveratively during his therapy sessions. In one session he stated that people who smoke and do not work will go to hell. I mused about his father's smoking and not working, wondering whether his father would go to hell. Mark matter-of-factly said that he would. When I asked Mark how he would feel about that, he promptly began to question me in his usual perseverative manner. I commented, "You ask me the same questions over and over again when I say something that makes you feel worried." Mark giggled delightedly and then promptly said no.

The focusing of the child's attention on his verbal communication differs from making a direct statement of the meaning behind the child's behavior. Drawing Mark's attention to his words was only a first step in a series of therapeutic interventions. A second level might aim at clarifying the interpersonal context. The therapist could comment, "When you say that your father will go to hell, it scares you because you think that makes you a bad boy, and no one would like you if you were bad." This intervention begins to focus the child on his more internal feeling states. While these interventions may help the child develop understanding into his functioning, insight is not a major intent for the intervention.

INTERPRETATION

Interpretation is a basic tool in the therapeutic process that encourages the therapeutic alliance, opens people to new experiences in and out of therapy, and effects changes in functioning (Lewis 1972). However, there are specific needs for the presentation of interpretations:

the presence of a positively established relationship between the child and the therapist

interpretations timed to enable the child to use the new
    information
wording of interpretations that are specific and concrete.

The child's defensive system is not the same as that of an adult
and hence unconscious connections are closer to consciousness and
repressions are less powerful.

Children often feel under attack when an observation or interpretation is made. They often respond to it as a criticism. Interpretations are also experienced as accusations, akin to all the other
blaming children experience from adults. Consequently there is a
strong resistance to interpretation.

The therapist usually obtains more material than can be used.
What is addressed or attended to by the therapist could therefore
be looked at as an interpretation even though it is not technically
considered one. In early sessions interpretations are not usually
made because there is not enough information available yet. Even
at first, when there is resistance, interpretations or more specifically reflections of behavior inform the child that you understand
his feelings. The source material from which an interpretation is
made is gathered from behaviors, dreams, stories, affects, drawings, waiting room behavior, and calls from parents and teacher.
However, children's material is not as clearly defined as adults',
so that interpretations are difficult to make in general. What children don't remember they may fill in with fantasies of what they
either feel the adult might want to hear or what they think happened. Information from parents and teachers can be useful, but
the information may reflect their views of what may be going on
with the child. We must deal with the behaviors of the child as
the primary source of data for our interpretations. The progression of an interpretation is important. Resistances and processes
are dealt with before defense, defense is handled before conflict,
and finally the conflict is interpreted. This progression becomes
impactful when the interventions made by the therapist arise from

the relationship between the therapist and the child and the material the child shares with the therapist.

TIMING

Timing is another critical step in the offering of an interpretation. The "right" time for the offering of an interpretation is when the interpretation will help consolidate gains and at the same time elicit new information. The dosage of an interpretive statement—how much understanding is shared with the child at a specific time in the therapeutic process—is also a function of timing, the relationship, and the child's developmental stage. Tact, timing, and dosage are the main factors that lead the therapist to effective interventions.

> Five-year-old Molly would respond to her therapist with "I already know that" whenever the therapist made any type of intervention. This was understood by the therapist as a resistance against intrusion. Molly had been sexually molested by her natural father for some two to three years when she visited him in his home. However, the issue was addressed not at the level of the conflict, that is, sexual pleasure, pain, intrusion and trauma, but rather at the level of the resistance and defense. When the therapist suggested that Molly likes to know everything by herself and be in control, the child readily agreed to the interpretation and then was able to ask the therapist for assistance.

The intervention reduced the youngster's defensiveness, did not interfere with the flow of the session, and permitted the child to use the therapist appropriately.

There are instances where tact may be contraindicated, for example, in being confrontative. Here the therapist may want to draw the child's attention to a behavior without explanation.

> Ten-year-old Aaron, during a game of Sorry, displayed poor strategy while verbalizing a strong need to win. His therapist commented that he sure seemed to be playing hard to lose.

In spite of Aaron's vigorous denial and his assertion that he really
wanted to win, his strategy during the game changed. The child
was able to use the attention-focusing statement and alter his
behavior.

Child therapy is a process that helps children resume development that had been waylaid by the vicissitudes of life within their
family. The therapist helps development resume by providing the
child with a relationship that is empathic and supportive. Toward
this end intrusiveness and extraction of information should not occur,
but the child should be invited to share whatever material he wishes.
Confrontations are experienced by the child as a violation of his
integrity. A direct question is experienced as a confrontation and
an expectation to give of an already impoverished store of childhood experiences. Furthermore, insights about past occurrences,
behaviors, and relationships are beyond the ability and contrary to
the developmental pushes of children across the childhood and early
adolescent years. Children have greater interest and investment in
the here-and-now aspects of their lives. Putting the past in perspective, understanding past relationships, and the ability to reflect upon
oneself are functions usually beyond the abilities of children. Preschoolers do not have a good sense of time partly because past and
present are merged and partly due to the ready regressions one often
sees with this age group. School-age children often have amnesia
for the preschool years and have no past to refer to. These children
are involved in the here-and-now aspects of their lives and expect
to arrive at solutions in the here and now. For the preadolescent
the past is revived in the present so that in essence here too is no
past. These aspects of children's functioning make the course of
treatment very different from the treatment of adults. Kennedy
(1977) states,

> When the child analyst understands the child's symbolic play but
> responds to it in an indirect way (either through play or verbal-

ization), the child will feel understood, although he will not gain
conscious awareness of what he is expressing. His feeling understood
may represent his past infantile experience of his mother's responding
appropriately with her more sophisticated understanding of his
needs. [p. 25]

The limits of children's understanding raise important questions regarding their ability to use interpretations therapists make
regarding behavior, motivation, and history. Shirk (1988) has suggested that a child's capacity to understand interpretations depends
on the child's cognitive development, the complexity of the interpretation, and the therapist's sensitivity to developmental as well as
psychological issues.

Generally, interpretations are made in the context of ongoing
therapy and are an outgrowth of the relationship that is developed
between the therapist and child and the material that has been presented. Interpretations are made in all forms of therapy, although they
will differ in substance and presentation depending on the personality organization and age of the patient and the theoretical orientation
of the therapist. Further, the level of cognitive and emotional development must be considered, as interpretations should not provide
children with information they would not have been expected to gain
given their developmental status. Therapeutic pacing is handled by
monitoring children's development via the complementary processes
of assimilation and accommodation (Piaget 1952). As therapists, we
need to know what understandings, attitudes, and beliefs the child
holds (assimilation) so that we can offer appropriate data to enable
the system to change and grow (accommodation).

> Jodi, 4 years old, was digging in the sandbox when she looked up
> and requested that I not let anyone touch her "hole" (the one she
> made in the sand). As I was not clear as to just what the concern
> was, I took a reality-oriented view and told her that I was not always
> in the playroom. Jodi reiterated that I should not let anyone touch

her hole even though I was not always in the playroom. It sounded as though Jodi thought that I had complete control over the happenings in the playroom, that perhaps I lived there. I addressed this issue and told her that I did not live in the playroom. She looked startled and asked me when I had moved.

Jodi and I went on to process this new information using the example that her mother worked but came home every night and lived in the house with Jodi and not at her place of work. I indicated that I worked in the playroom but went home to my own house when I was finished working. Once she was able to fully understand the issue of where I lived, we were able to move on and deal with the issue of masturbation and anatomical differences between boys and girls, which were secondary issues in her request for protection of her hole. Assimilation and accommodation, while important processes to consider in any treatment, are not the only issues that must be considered when making an interpretation. The therapist must have a working knowledge of the thinking processes of children as they too must be considered when making interpretations over the course of therapy.

Some of the resistances seen in child therapy may reflect the limitations of the child's understanding of psychological causality. However, children will integrate those interpretations they can understand.

Interpretations must match the cognitive level of the specific child and be close to the understandings that the child had already established. Further, children at all ages engage in all-or-nothing behavior. Thus, if they lose a game, not only are they a bad game player, but also they are bad across all aspects of functioning. Conversely, if they win, they are good across the board. While this cognitive stance is most obvious in the preschool and early school-age child, it resurfaces each time a child grows into a new developmental level. Understanding the cognitive and emotional development will make interpretation more effective.

INTERPRETATION FOR PRESCHOOLERS

Preschoolers are very concrete, egocentric thinkers whose understandings of the world are heavily affected by visual inputs. They are convinced that everyone has the same thoughts as themselves and must actively play out their thinking processes repetitively to gain an understanding/resolution of the dilemmas with which they are trying to cope. They often confuse wishes and reality, which interferes with logical thinking. Because of their high level of egocentricity, they are unable to think about themselves or to put themselves in the place of others.

> Jamie, 3 years, 3 months old, was referred for therapy because of "hyperactive" behavior following a minor car accident in which his chin was cut. During one session Jamie explained to his therapist that he was sitting in the front seat and the car hit another car and he bumped his chin and "Mommy put a diaper under my chin cause it was bleeding." As the child described the incident he became more and more agitated and seemed nearly ready to bolt the room. His therapist commented on how frightened he must have been, especially since he thought he had hurt his penis. Jamie readily responded to his therapist's understanding of his feelings and his castration concerns. His relief was temporary, however, and his anxiety began building again as he wondered out loud when he got his penis. (He has a sister who is 18 months old.) Jamie first thought that he had gotten his penis last week, then said when he had his third birthday, then he decided he got it when he was a baby. Not one of the dates he proposed seemed to satisfy the child. His therapist told him that a boy is born with his penis. Jamie's glee and relief were immediately evident and he bounded out of the playroom to share this newfound information with his mother, the secretary, and anyone else in the waiting room.

Within this vignette the reader can find both interpretation (e.g., castration fears) and educative responses (e.g., boys are born with their penises). The interplay of explanation and new information is an important feature of all therapy. Explanations help children to understand issues they are trying to deal with, while new information is an aid toward growth. The session with Jamie was unusual by virtue of the fact that it was primarily verbal. More typically, preschoolers express their thinking, worrying, and fantasies in play.

Play is an expression of children's thinking processes externally presented. In addition, play segments can be repeated with alternative endings, giving them a problem-solving potential. These are major reasons for play being the treatment modality of choice for children. Additional reasons for the use of play in treatment include:

little or no capacity for self observation,
no reversibility in their thinking so that reconstructive work
    is difficult,
limited vocabulary and/or means (concepts) to describe ordinary events of life,
no real differentiation of inner experiences and outer reality.

Nevertheless, we can develop a meaningful working alliance with these young children, handle their transferences and resistances, and make interpretations.

> Each time 4-year-old Joel was in the playroom he approached the dollhouse, found the "mother doll," looked under her dress, sat her on the toilet, and then proceeded to an activity where he could establish his competence and beginning identification as a male. My first intervention was to describe what the child was doing behaviorally. In my second intervention I suggested that Joel wondered what the mother doll looked like underneath her dress, and in my third intervention I suggested that he might be curious about the difference between boys and girls. At this point, the use of the anatomically correct dolls in the playroom served to help Joel understand that girls have vaginas and boys have penises. The fourth and final time Joel played this theme out, he firmly sat the

mother doll on the toilet seat and I responded that "ladies go potty sitting down but boys go potty standing up," to which he replied "yup" and went to the sandbox to "plant a garden." Until this session Joel talked about being a farmer like his maternal grandfather, but during this session he announced he was going to be a farmer like his father.

The response to Joel's play on the symbolic level he presented, rather than on the concrete level of "mother doll" equals mother, allowed him to deal with male–female differences, oedipal struggles, and identification in his own way, without the intrusion of age-inappropriate understanding of his struggles. This more subtle approach to therapeutic intervention helped to facilitate the development of coping strategies based on the child's own struggles, rather than on the unwarranted intrusions of an adult. Interventions, especially with children, need to be parsimonious, and need not provide children with a complete or comprehensive explanation of their productions and functioning in order to resolve problems and effect changes.

INTERPRETATION FOR SCHOOL-AGERS

When treating school-age children it is important to keep in mind that the aims of psychotherapy and the aims of this developmental period conflict. Bornstein (1948) stressed the importance of a child's defenses as a protection against impulses. Thus, the therapist must respect the resistances of the child. The defenses are slowly and tactfully dealt with throughout the therapeutic process.

> Ten-year-old Scott would repeatedly tell me I was wrong each time I made a comment or outright interpretation. Initially I would let his denial stand. As time went on and I continued to be wrong, I would then comment on how I did not seem to understand what he was trying to tell me and that it usually led to my being wrong.

He would reassure me that I was sometimes right, only this time I
was wrong.

   During the second year of treatment I made an interpretation,
to which he replied, as usual, that I was wrong. I told him that this
time I was not wrong. He became quite angry and asked if I ever
thought that I could be wrong. He was taken aback when I told
him that I thought about it all the time.

Scott's reactions not only give us an example of defense resistance,
but at the same time indicate that earlier, denied interpretations/
interventions had been accepted by the child without conscious
acknowledgment. Confrontation of the child's resistances to interventions was not attempted for a long time.

   Twelve-year-old Martine would reply no to each intervention,
reformulation of her statement, or interpretation of her stories. After
some weeks of this response from her I had the distinct impression
that her no was an important communication. Thus, I asked her
how old was she telling me she was. She promptly replied, "Two."
When I commented that if she were two she would not have been
molested by her uncle, she shook her head in agreement and
proceeded to demonstrate how a two-year-old acted.

Martine was able to approach the very shameful experience of her
sexual molestation, which she had been avoiding through her resistance not only to intervention but also to involvement in a therapeutic relationship.

   Enabling the child to play out conflicts through the use of
drawings and paintings, telling stories, and relating dreams and daydreams may help circumvent the resistances latency-aged children
erect against the therapeutic process. Klein (1975) felt that daydreams
were an expression of the child's unconscious and could therefore
be of help in dealing with the child's conflicts. Sarnoff (1976) suggests that slips of the tongue, often used by the latency-aged child
as confirmation of interpretations and a breakthrough of unconscious
or consciously concealed material, should be addressed immediately.

Children of these ages are often intrigued by these slips of the tongue. They are able to understand their dual level of meaning and can be intrigued by their production.

Therapy with the latency-aged child, while similar to that with other age groups, has its own specific problems. The normal style of pathological-like behavior makes the school-aged child difficult to evaluate initially as well as during the course of treatment. His style of communication is foreign to the adult; babbling on and on, playing out one fantasy after another, and jumping from one developmental level to another without any apparent precipitating causes. Further, the child of this developmental level does not have future planning ability. Thus, he needs to be reminded, in different therapy contexts, of the reasons he is being seen.

A further difficulty for the treatment process during latency results from the contradictory processes of this age and the aims of therapy. During latency, the developmental focus moves from internal to external processes, while the intent of psychotherapy is to move from external to internal processes. However, the playroom and all its equipment often encourage the externalization of self-perception, perception of others, and interpersonal relationships. While school- or latency-age children are quite resistant to revealing their internal processes, they are usually expressed through their choices and the ways in which play materials are used.

> Nine-year-old Terry, in her second year of therapy, chose to play checkers after three months of exhibiting an approach-avoidance set of behaviors related to board games. Before the game was completely over she said that she wanted to stop. I responded to her request stating, "It is hard to lose." Terry responded in turn with the observation that I was a good player. She was able to complete the game, even though she lost as she expected.

Terry's approach-avoidance was an expression of the dilemma children in the latency period are constantly struggling with, to win or lose, to fight or flee. How children resolve these conflicting pulls during this level of development provides them with the beginning coping strategies that will be used throughout their lives. In the vignette presented above, my intervention allowed Terry to complete the game even though it was clearly apparent to both of us that she would not win. In ensuing games, I gave myself a handicap to reduce the discrepancy between our skills. The child continued to lose. Her inability to win a game was based on issues other than skill.

Latency-aged children are difficult to treat. They have come out of the preschool years with some minimal controls over impulses that were hard won and hence they are not going to readily explore their internal states and put their hard-won controls in jeopardy. The defenses they have been able to erect are a protection against those barely-under-control impulses. If the therapist pushes against these defenses, they usually increase in strength. Therefore, the therapist must respect these defenses and the children's resistances. Latency-aged children externalize their conflicts. It is through this externalization that therapy can be accomplished.

> Ten-year-old Greg was brought to therapy because of a depression severe enough for him to have considered suicide. His parents divorced when he was 5 and he had been living with his mother and younger sister. He saw his father regularly and seemed to have a good relationship with him. While he was quite resistive to being in therapy, during the first session he built a tennis court out of wood and other materials available for his use in the playroom. He also created two players, each holding a racquet, one of whom had a ball. Wordlessly the youngster showed me what he had made. I shared with him my impression and proceeded to describe the players, the tennis racquet, and the ball, including the possibility that the players can sure parry the ball back and forth. As I described his creation he smiled and nodded, as though he were pleased that I understood his production.

The youngster's behavior suggested that he felt caught in the middle of his divorced parents' conflicts and was in their control, unable to establish controls for himself. Being brought to therapy was another instance of his being in parental control. Greg's resistance to therapy could not be reduced no matter what intervention was offered to him. He needed to deal with the issue of control directly with his parents, whose conflicts with one another kept this child trapped in his situation. Given the nature of his feelings, the immediate reality problems, and his resistance, family therapy was recommended.

> Eleven-year-old Lara was seen in therapy because of issues revolving around being a girl. She came from a family of religious fundamentalists and was enrolled in a one-room, K–12 Christian school. She had an older brother who had more freedoms than she was allowed. Her status, as was her mother's, was inferior to the men of the family and both seemed to resent their positions. I had a hunch that the mother was using the child as a way of entering therapy for herself. However, the child had issues of her own that were being addressed by the therapy. Within the first ten sessions Lara played with the nursing bottle in the playroom. After a number of false starts, the child, in an embarrassed manner, brought the nipple to her mouth. The therapist commented that it seemed as though she [Lara] was trying to remember what it felt like when she was a baby. The child's embarrassment was reduced and she was then able to vigorously suck on the nipple. The interpretation that Lara wished to become a baby again as a way of starting out as a boy this time was not made.

Comments and fantasies about the advantages of being male had a greater likelihood of being stated as the therapy progressed due to the therapist's benign acceptance of the regressed behavior without linking the overt behavior to the covert wishes.

CONDUCT DISORDERS

Conduct disorders in childhood are a variant of character disorders and represent a freezing of the personality structure, which interferes with the slow evolution of personality structure. Fluidity of personality organization in children is necessary to allow for their slow evolution into adulthood. The basic guidelines of child therapy described above can be used with these more rigid and disturbed children. As these conduct-disordered children do not tolerate anxiety very well, it is necessary for the therapist to manage the anxiety level of the child. These children enact their anxieties against an environment that has not set standards of behavior to which these children are held. They in turn feel deprived of the basic satisfaction of their needs. The acting-out behaviors of these children are their way of involving the environment in interaction as well as avoiding despair over ever having their needs met. Small doses of anxiety may be tolerated by conduct-disordered children as they deal with their desperation regarding need satisfaction. The therapist must behave in a reliable, trustworthy fashion with consistency and clear limit setting. While these features are necessary in all forms of therapy, they are especially important with the conduct-disordered child. If the therapist yields or bends the rules to meet the demands of the youngster in an attempt to avoid an explosive episode, greater loss of control and more demanding behavior are the outcome.

> Brett, 11 years old, was as tall as I and twenty-five pounds heavier. His ability to push me around was quite real, especially when his behavior was out of control. My therapeutic interventions were presented either gingerly or not at all to avoid the eruption of his anger. Interpretations of his self-hate were the usual trigger to aggressive acting out, and inevitably he did lose control. At those times he would throw things toward me and become very intimidating. Verbal interventions and/or interpretations had no impact on the escalating behaviors. I would complete the session with him and he would follow me down to my office where he was prepared to continue his harassing behaviors. Gradually, since verbal interventions had no apparent impact on this youngster, I would end the session prematurely, with explanations for my actions, once his behavior began to escalate. He would still follow me to my office, but now he would apologize

profusely for his behaviors and explain that he did not understand why he had acted as he had. We would finish the session in my office in spite of the fact that I had just previously terminated the session because of his problematic behavior in the playroom. Exploration of his playroom behavior did not ameliorate the situation. During one particularly difficult session, Brett's behavior was so problematic that I once again terminated the session. When he followed me back to my office and apologized profusely I told him that I would not accept his apology this time. He was surprised and told me that his father always did so. I explained that when people apologized they meant that not only were they truly sorry that they had behaved badly, but also that they were going to try and do better, to change their behavior the next time. I further stated that he seemed to think that an apology wiped out the "bad" behavior and then he didn't have to worry or think about it any more and also that he didn't have to do anything differently. He agreed with me, and seemed genuinely surprised that he was expected to behave differently after he had said he was sorry. I told him I wouldn't accept his apologies on that basis anymore, but would expect him to behave differently. Brett left my office and waited in the waiting room until his session would have been over, something he had not done before.

After this encounter, Brett's behavior was under better control. When his unacceptable behavior began to escalate, verbal interventions were more effective in helping him resume control. Intervention rather than avoidance was more effective in dealing with this child's threatening behavior. My intervention seemed to have been received by Brett as my willingness to be involved in a relationship with him and not be pushed away. His behavior with peers and other adults consistently resulted in rejection for him, but now he found someone who would not reject him.

Much has been said of the prognostic implications of the presence or absence of anxiety in conduct disorders. Many theorists have considered that if the symptoms are ego-syntonic, then the person is devoid of anxiety, with no motivation to change. Certainly, many of these children are resentful and suspicious of any interference by an adult. However, behind the structure of the defenses, there lie great anger, self-doubt, conflict, and anxiety. These feelings are usually enacted within the environment, rather than expressed through verbal or imaginative modalities. It is the task of the therapist, via the relationship, to help the child learn how to deal with his anxieties as well as the wide range of feelings we all experience. Helping conduct-disordered children learn that their needs will be met, their feelings understood, and their person respected will motivate them toward change and growth.

SUMMARY

In general, effective intervention strengthens the therapeutic relationship and alliance and enables psychological, behavioral, and cognitive changes to occur. These effects are accomplished through the sensitive and tactful symbolic, behavioral, and verbal responses of the therapist to the often obscure communications of the child. As Ginott (1968) stated, "The role of the therapist is to comprehend play language and to communicate his understanding to the child. The child's play message and the adult's verbal decoding become a healing dialogue" (p. 40).

Lewis (1972) has suggested a number of subdivisions for interpretation with children:

1. Setting statements: conditions for the treatment to occur (e.g., no hurting the therapist, oneself, or the deliberate destruction of toys; time and days of sessions; cancellation of sessions; confidentiality; communication with guardians) and the reasons the child is being seen in treatment from both the adult's and the child's point of view.
2. Attention statements: drawing the child's attention to his activities and verbalizations and/or providing a verbal com-

mentary to the play behavior but not necessarily drawing connections between fantasy and reality.

3. Reductive statements: drawing connections between overtly disparate comments, behaviors, and ideas.

4. Situational statements: how specific interactions give rise to specific patterns of behavior.

5. Transference statements: these are quite problematic in child therapy. The field in general is in conflict between those therapists who assert that transferences do not occur and those who assert that transferences are obtained in child therapy. The most likely transferential response from a child will be a simple displacement from the parents (e.g., "You are just like my mother"). It is this type of response, from the child, that is responded to and interpreted, within the current reality context.

6. Etiological statements: links between current behavior and past experiences. However, the child needs to be in later phases of latency in order to understand this form of inter-pretation.

Intervention in child treatment need not be as formalized as has been presented so far. The child can learn and grow from experiencing an adult respond to him in different and unexpected ways from what the child has come to expect from other adults in the environment. The new response often has a growth-enhancing aspect to it that should not be underestimated as an important aspect of the therapeutic process. However, the therapist must consider that the internal and external world of thoughts, emotions, ideas, and memories the child has is part of the therapeutic process of every session.

7

RESISTANCES TO CHILD THERAPY

R esistance to the therapeutic process was described by Freud (1905) and many subsequent therapists as a rejection by the patient of the therapist's care and concern. This rejection often results in retaliation by the therapist blaming the patient. However, resistance characterizes the patient's attempts to protect herself from psychotherapeutic interventions that may well be insensitive or an error. Blaming the patient is easier than looking at one's own therapeutic errors. Responding improperly is inevitable in all interpersonal relationships and leads to counterreactions. Thus, these resistances are a familiar response in treatment with both adults and children.

As children's defenses do not have the rigidity or solidity of adult defenses, their protests are often stronger, more pervasive, and more implacable. The child may experience the therapist and the therapeutic setting as an intrusive and threatening encounter demanding an all-out defense. This intense reaction occurs in part because children rarely ask for therapy. The child comes fearfully, wondering if something will be done to her against her will. Depending on the degree of emotional difficulty, and experiences with adults, the child may perceive and respond to the therapist as trying to control and/or dominate her. Even if the child does not view the therapist as another intrusive and dangerous adult, the material produced through the therapeutic interaction provokes feelings and ideas that the child fears may overwhelm her. The child resists exposing those parts of herself that upset equilibrium and stability. Because of the therapeutic focus on the very conflicts the child is defending against and the intense level of anxiety surrounding the issue, the child will use whatever means necessary to deflect attention from these vital issues. This may appear, at times, to be negativistic or oppositional on the child's part.

> The mother of 8-year-old Tom told me she had found some of her Tampax and sanitary pads in his room. When I raised this with Tom in session he turned his back to me announcing he was not going to talk about it and he was just going to ignore me. This is a youngster who characteristically shared his thoughts and feelings on a very symbolic level. My interventions usually remained on this level, allowing him to take them in and incorporate them. This current communication was handled directly and to the issue. I could appreciate Tom's refusal to engage with me over this issue. He looked wounded by my confrontation, which suggested to me that something had to be done right then to repair the rupture in the relationship. I suggested that he had taken these things of his mother's because he had a question he did not know how to put into words. He agreed with me but could not explain his dilemma further. I suggested that he wondered about the differences between boys and girls and how babies were made. He again nodded, but this time he seemed more relaxed than when we began this disquieting session.

While there are other basic issues to this child's taking of his mother's sanitary products my intervention gave him the opportunity to alter his apparent expectation that he would be made to feel like a "bad" boy.

The child is often fully aware of the extent to which she is resisting and even of the conflictual material being avoided. The child may deliberately choose to avoid discussing particular issues and may consciously withhold information, as in the vignette above, or offer fabricated stories.

> Jerry was brought into therapy because of the emotional turmoil he was experiencing in the fourth grade classroom of an overtly sadistic teacher. The therapist, in an attempt to monitor the child's experience, asked him at the beginning of one session, "How was school?" He replied, "Fine." The therapist responded to the "resistance" with, "Are you saying fine because school was really O.K. or because I am just another adult who thinks school is always fine for kids and that's what I want to hear?" Jerry agreed that he said fine because that's what he thought the therapist wanted to hear and then was able to describe the current day's traumas.

While the child may not be aware of her reluctance to share with the therapist, it may be recognized by the child when her attention is focused on the avoidance of an issue. (The child's resistance presents itself at various levels of consciousness and at various points during the therapeutic process.)

address it!

Some children will be persistent in their efforts to avoid specific therapeutic interventions, while others will present more transient or intermittent forms of resistance. It is important to note that particular behaviors may serve as resistive measures for the child. At other times the same behaviors may have a different meaning.

> Seven-year-old Eddie was brought to the therapist by his separating parents because of aggressive behavior both at school and at home. Early in treatment Eddie repetitively played out a chase theme where the small boy doll always outwitted the bigger policemen. Each time I made a comment about the play sequence it interfered with the play and led Eddie to wander about the playroom aimlessly.
>   Toward the end of treatment Eddie played out a similar aggressive theme with his back to me as he quietly verbalized the

interactions between his characters. Now he used either action figures or miniature soldiers. He occasionally told me what he was doing or invited me over to see how he had set up his forces in the sandbox. At the end of one play sequence that included a long drawn out battle I asked him who had won. He looked at me in surprise and said, "The good guys, of course."

During the early phase of treatment he kept me out of his play so that he would not have to learn about his anger toward his father who was an intrusive, controlling, and angry man who responded to his son unempathically. The similar behavior toward the end of treatment reflects this child's appropriate latency struggles with aggression and his beginning development of the capacity to be alone (Winnicott 1958).

The pattern and intensity of resistance can tell much about the aspects of the child's experience with which the therapist must be concerned. The therapeutic task is to recognize the child's resistance as it presents itself in the interaction. Assessment of the intensity of the resistance and its role in the child's current functioning must also be addressed.

Eleven-year-old Sally had been voicing anger about being in therapy. Even though her current difficulties in interpersonal relationships and her problems with her mother were presented as the reasons for treatment, she insisted that she had had "counseling" for a long time and she no longer wanted to come. The therapist had been interpreting Sally's hostility and what it does to her relationships with peers and adults. Sally was resistant to whatever the therapist presented in terms of an explanation. She could only see her particular point of view. Supervision helped the therapist take another tack with this child. The therapist pulled back during sessions, remaining available but quiet and responding only when the child asked for something directly. Within the session following this change in tactic Sally began telling the therapist about the particulars of her peer interactions and how much she "hated" herself. Two sessions later the child said that it really wasn't so bad coming to treatment, and she even liked the playroom.

Once the therapist could understand the needs of the child and respond accordingly, the resistance dropped away. More of the conflictual material began to arise, leading to the possibility of it being resolved.

At the beginning of this chapter I suggested that resistance was a result of a difficulty in the therapeutic dyad and here I am intimating that resistance arises out of the difficulties of the child. Both points of view are important to consider. Children can and do consciously withhold information that would be important to explore. However, we must always take into consideration not only the cognitive processes available to the child but also our own reactions to the child's behavior. When we do, it becomes apparent that children do not think like adults and that their thinking processes often take them into difficult dead ends. On the other side, we may recognize our anger with the child's behavior, such as resisting the treatment process, especially our interventions. LaClave and Brack (1989) suggest that reframing an issue raised by a patient changes the way in which it is viewed not only by the patient but the therapist as well. If we look at a patient issue as a resistance to the therapist and therapeutic process, we gear up to "attack" or get rid of something that is unwanted, at least to the therapist. However, if we look at the coping skills behind the resistance we will probably approach the issue from a more positive stance.

Coping not resistance

At the end of the first year of treatment Sarah did not want to come anymore. She gave her mother a hard time when it was time for her appointment. When she entered the playroom, she was silent and sullen, often doing nothing for long periods of time. She said she would come, but not on a school day or whenever she had something else planned. I explained that I could not agree to that, but that if she really did not want to come we could stop the appointments, and that I would see her one more time when school started. I was about to go on vacation, which allowed for this mini-termination. In the fall she returned for that one session and told me she wanted to keep coming. When she was really ready for termination she told me that she no longer felt she had to come as she did earlier in treatment. Further, she now feels good when she starts the session and feels good when she ends the session, whereas before she felt terrible at the beginning and good when she left.

The sticking point for this child was her anger with her mother. Her pleasure in the expression of anger both exhilarated and frightened her. She was able to approach this issue by first talking about her pleasure with her anger toward her younger sister, then she could deal with her feelings toward her mother. The summer break from treatment, with the knowledge that I would not force her back into treatment, and the issues that frightened her allowed her to approach her problems at her own pace. I did not label her requests as resistance, and I responded to her unreasonable demands in a realistic manner. Thus she was able to experience me as noncoercive and in that way I was different from the other adults she has known. Just as a child's resistance presents itself at various levels of consciousness and at various points during the therapeutic process, so, too, we see the characteristics of resistance manifested in a variety of ways. Some children are persistent in their efforts to avoid therapeutic intervention, while others present more transient or intermittent forms of resistance.

> Eleven-year-old Robin was brought to therapy by her seriously depressed mother because of the child's demanding behavior. Robin's father was not involved in a relationship with either mother or child and it seemed likely that divorce was in the offing. While the child enjoyed being with the therapist during the evaluation sessions, she absolutely refused to come to treatment. Her protest was based on her need to have a direct, emotional relationship with her mother and her refusal to have any substitute. The demand was for her mother's involvement and was not considered a resistance to therapy per se.

It is important to reiterate that while particular behaviors may at one time serve as resistive measures, for the child the same behaviors may have a different significance at other points in therapy.

Resistance is a phenomenon (1) that is encountered by all therapists throughout the course of treatment regardless of the approach to treatment, because miscommunication and misunderstanding are inevitable in all relationships; (2) that occurs with considerable variety in terms of the degree of anxiety the material in question provokes for the child and the level of consciousness at which it is manifested; (3) that can be a therapeutic tool rather than a hindrance to treatment; and (4) that can tell much about the aspects of the child's experience to which the therapist must be more sensitive.

Thus, the therapist's task is to recognize the child's resistance as it presents itself in the therapeutic interaction and assess the intensity, as well as the role, of the resistance in the child's current functioning. Eventually, the conflictual material and experiences that are being kept from full awareness can be identified and the misunderstanding between therapist and patient can be repaired. The therapeutic management of resistance will be a function of the style of the therapist, the type of treatment, the timing of the intervention, the age of the child, and the overall strategy of therapy.

RESISTANCE DURING THE PRESCHOOL YEARS

The most common forms of resistance seen during the preschool years are a refusal to enter the playroom without a parent, a refusal to play or talk, ignoring the therapist's comments, pushing toys away, feigned inadequacy (saying "I can't" or "I don't know" when it is apparent that she does), and oppositional behavior. All of these behaviors are indicative of the child's attempts to deal with the unavoidable stress involved in dealing with a new environment and an unknown adult. The resistance of the preschool child is direct, overt, and easy to understand.

During a play group composed of six children ranging in age from 4 to 6, and two therapists, one youngster giggled and squirmed when she undressed her baby doll and discovered that the doll had a penis. The therapist took note of this reaction, and commented on physical differences between boys and girls and the different feelings people have about their bodies. As this discussion unfolded, the same child heard chimes ringing outside and noted, "Oops! I guess it's time for group to be over."

The group was fifteen minutes into an hour-and-a-half session. The sexual material that was raised seems to have generated much anxiety in the children. One way of avoiding the discomfort was to leave the group.

RESISTANCE DURING THE SCHOOL YEARS

During the school years children typically become more sophisticated in their resistances. While each child develops resistances based on her unique history, there are some general resistances expressed by a wide range of school-aged children:

1. Symptom intensification—the anxiety generated in therapy propels the child to put more energy into an established pattern of behavior that has warded off anxiety in the past.
2. Selective inattention—the child ignores material brought out through therapeutic activity. This material has anxiety closely tied to it and we may see the child become attentive to interactions devoid of the conflictual material.
3. Silence or lulling—the child ignores and/or avoids the therapist during the session. Although it may signal a more reluctant child in the initial stage of treatment, it may also occur at junctures when conflictual material is being

aroused and there is an attempt on the child's part to divert treatment.

4. Inability to recall—the child fails to remember the last session or clarifications made during the session.

5. Somatic complaints—the child expresses somatic concerns that often are expressive of or in response to the conflictual material brought up in the sessions.

6. Transference resistance—the therapist activates the child's attitudes and feelings about parents directly. The child's defenses are provoked and she will attempt to alleviate the anxiety through (a) detaching herself from therapy, (b) attempting to control the therapy or therapist, (c) establishing herself as invincible and powerful.

7. Flight into health—the child's attempts to convince the therapist and herself that treatment is not needed. The symptoms the child came for may be under tight control and seem to have disappeared.

8. Self degradation—the child presents a hopeless, worthless image of herself relating that therapy cannot help. The child maintains a contemptible self concept that serves to deflect blame from the love object. This might also provide the child protection from critical assault from others.

9. Separating treatment from outside life—although the child appears to work hard in therapy and gain understanding there is little or no carryover into outside life.

10. Acting out—the child is unwilling or unable to verbalize and express feelings other than in activities that reenact the problems. This occurs within therapy as well as outside and tends to support the child's inability to express her/his feelings verbally. The behavior drains off psychic energy and leaves little left for therapeutic work.

11. Play interruption—unconscious material becomes conscious prematurely, as seen in the following vignette:

Eight-year-old Ruth was brought into therapy because of difficulty with all aspects of learning, oppositional behavior, and enuresis. A much wanted and favored younger brother displaced her as the "baby" of the family, resulting in deep resentment and much hostility. In one session, Ruth played with a small dollhouse with a detachable chimney. In her family play sequence the little boy of the family climbed out upon the roof and leaned (hid) against the chimney. As she let go of the doll, the chimney gave way and the doll fell to the table, on its back, arms outstretched. Ruth blanched and immediately left the playroom to go to the bathroom. When she returned, she chose another quiet activity. The therapist alleviated Ruth's anxiety by commenting neither upon her fright nor upon how real it looked. The "accident" was too close to her wish to deal with the material.

HANDLING THE RESISTANCE

I received a message from 12-year-old John, canceling his session 10 minutes before its beginning due to illness. As the message was out of character for previously received similar messages, I called his home. His mother said that John had told her I had called canceling the session. Clarifying the youngster's maneuver, she agreed to bring him to my office right away.

> As John entered my office it was obvious that he was angry. His resistance was apparent in the messages he left for his mother and myself. Having been thwarted, the anger that was being expressed looked as though it would be used for more resistance; it needed to be handled immediately.
>
> I felt that John was ashamed at having been caught dealing dishonestly with his mother and myself and that his self-esteem was at a low ebb. I therefore supported the resistance. I told him that I thought that he pulled a good stunt and that I was impressed with the way he carried the whole thing off. John's face brightened, his

body relaxed, he giggled, and with some minor questioning went on to explain how he thought up the whole incident and why he did not want to be at the day's session.

The child comes to therapy with a history of defenses and evasive patterns to defend against anxiety that has been overwhelming. Therapy provokes the reexperiencing of these conflicts. In the face of resistive behaviors, therapeutic success depends primarily on the therapist's willingness and ability to be receptive to the intense feelings of the child, especially to the child's projection of fear, aggression, and despair. In this, the therapist must provide a manageable context to the child's capacity to reevaluate and reassess her distortions of the experience by comparing internal pictures of the world with reality. Therefore, strategies for handling resistance call for gradual reduction of the intensity of the anxiety so that conflicts previously defended against may emerge into consciousness and be subject to conscious integration. Initial steps are focused on helping the child recognize the resistance being manifested and pointing to the nature of the resistance as well as the specific function. Eventually, the therapist can begin to identify the conflicts to which the child is resistant and help her to recognize and resolve them.

Whether one deals with children or adults there are four broad methods of dealing with resistance: joining it, mirroring it, confronting it, and clarifying its existence (Marshall 1982).

1. *Joining the resistance* refers to any move on the part of the therapist that gives the client permission to be resistant, as in the vignette above with John. This does not overtly challenge the defensive structure, and as a result of the unexpected response allows the child to cautiously explore what is being defended against.
2. *Mirroring the resistance* involves reflecting the emotions expressed by the child, which gives the child the freedom to become comfortable within the relationship.

Alice, 9 years old, had asked her mother to take her to see a psychologist because of distressing thoughts of either killing herself or killing her mother. I raised this with Alice during our initial session as this was the presenting problem and consciously available material. The youngster's anxiety climbed and she looked quite uncomfortable. I reflected her fear and reluctance to talk about her ideations, which provided her with some relief. This allowed her to explore the playroom, become involved in an activity, and question me about my experience in working with children. I had made an error and she was certainly informing me of it by her question.

3. *Confronting the resistance* forces the child's attention on the resistance itself.

May, a 9-year-old who was seen in twice-weekly therapy, frequently responded with "I don't know" or "kinda" whenever emotion-laden subjects were brought up. During one such discussion in which feelings of anger were explored, she interrupted the discussion by suggesting a game. The game consisted of timing the therapist to see how long she (the therapist) could remain completely silent. The therapist kept quiet, but wrote on the blackboard, "If I don't talk, then you don't have to hear anything upsetting." The child responded affirmatively, nevertheless, the game continued for the remainder of the session.

4. *Clarifying the resistance* helps the child to understand the resistance. This understanding breaks up the resistance and usually allows the child to proceed with working through conflictual material.

Gary, mentioned in previous chapters, lay down on the floor making angels in the rug (a game akin to angels in the snow) when termination was raised. Each time this issue was raised resistive maneuvers arose, making any discussion impossible. The therapist, after letting the resistance develop over a number of sessions, interpreted it. In part, Gary's resistance was an attempt to master all the previous separations he had experienced in his life over which he had no control. The youngest of five children in his natural family, he was left in an infant bassinet all day long with no attention to his physical or emotional needs. The authorities removed him from the home because of neglect, and parental rights were terminated. At age 11 months to 2 years he was placed in three foster homes until he was adopted. There was much marital strife including separation and reconciliation of the couple over the next four years when the adoptive mother left, leaving Gary with his father. She reentered the child's life seeking full custody when he was 9.

Gary's resistance was related to his attempt to have control over the separation (from the therapist) as well as a defense against the upsurge of feelings related to his sense of being bad and the cause of all the other separations he had previously experienced. In a subsequent session, as termination was again touched upon and Gary used diversionary tactics to avoid the issue, the therapist commented on how difficult it was to say good-bye when he had been given away so many times when he was very little. Gary was quite responsive to the interpretation and was able to express anger toward his adoptive mother for having left him as well as acceptance and understanding of his last foster mother's relinquishment of him. The child and therapist were thus able to move ahead and discuss termination.

As was mentioned earlier, resistance is an inevitable part of the therapeutic process and does not depend on the age of the client or the sensitivity of the therapist. However, children have ways of resisting that differ from adults. The preschooler cannot be separated from the mother, who then must be included in the playroom and becomes an integral part of the therapy. For the young (6–10) school-aged child thoughts and feelings become an issue. The child wonders if she is crazy and/or different from other kids. She is afraid the therapist will "read my mind" and find out about these crazy thoughts and so she looks away from the therapist. She is also afraid that the other kids will find out she is seeing a "shrink" and taunt her about it. The 10- to 12-year-old, preparing for adolescence,

becomes involved in masturbatory behavior and fears that the therapist will find out about this and punish her. To release some of the
sexual tension the child is beginning to feel, she often feels the
need to be in constant motion and constantly doing something.
This makes it difficult for the therapist to follow the train of
thought or to concentrate on what is being done. In this way the
10- to 12-year-old feels she can keep the therapist from "finding
out about me." Because the child does not, in most cases, willingly
bring herself to therapy, she does not feel committed to giving the
therapist information about herself. The therapist is still seen as an
authority figure, against whom the child needs to defend herself. A
power struggle can follow, interfering with the treatment process
until the therapist and child realize that there really isn't a power
struggle at all.

The child needs time to decide that she can trust the therapist
not to tell parents about the "bad" things that she has thought or
done. But even when the child comes to trust the therapist not to
tell, she may be torn by mixed loyalties at times. The child may
feel that she is "telling" on parents if they're fighting or other behavior that is bothering her is discussed with the therapist. For this
reason, the therapist needs the cooperation of the parents to tell the
child that it's all right to discuss with the therapist anything that is
troubling her. The child may also feel that by not talking about
frightening thoughts and feelings, they will cease to exist. When
the therapist alludes to these frightening thoughts and feelings, the
child may ignore her, cover her own ears, or even threaten to leave
and never come back. In this way the child attempts to protect what
she works so hard to defend against.

Another issue in the treatment of children is the value-laden
terms used in discipline. "Good" means submitting and conforming to adult expectations and "bad" refers to rebellion and defiance
of adult authority, with the latter to be followed by some form of
punishment. The implication is that part of the child is bad and the

punishment is aimed at eradicating that unacceptable part of the child. The child needs help in separating out her behavior from her value as a person. As the differences are explored and experienced by the child, she may be distrustful of the therapist, thinking that she has done things that are so bad that the therapist needs to find a way to deny it. The therapist may be seen by the child as the "final effort" to change her and therefore can be experienced as more powerful and dangerous than other adults. The child may also wonder to what extent the therapist will force conformity. She may have heard of hypnosis, brain surgery, electroshock devices, and medications—all extreme, last-chance efforts to force the child to do what others want of her. This would be especially threatening to the child if she views conforming as a loss of identity and an annihilation of individuality. The child would feel the need to keep her distance from the therapist in order to keep from being devoured.

PARENTAL RESISTANCE

The parents may also play a very important role in resistance to treatment. One of the reactions the parents have to emotionally disturbed children is guilt. Parents may fluctuate between feeling responsible for the child's problems and denying that responsibility by finding something or someone to blame, such as heredity or the therapist for not being able to immediately "make him better." This may be an impetus for the parents to prematurely pull the child out of therapy. Parents need to have the guilt lifted from their shoulders by assuring them that they are doing the best they can for the child and are looking after the child's needs by bringing her for therapy.

Rather than pulling the child out of therapy, parents may also effectively undermine therapy. They often cannot tolerate the therapist as a "better parent" than they are, succeeding in winning the child's respect and trust where they have failed. It may also be that the parent actually does not want the child to get better for reasons such as keeping the child from growing up, or that a problematic child will keep the focus off of a very troubled marriage.

The parents need to feel that they are helping their child directly. Regular parent conferences focusing on parent feelings about the child, and alternative child-rearing practices and ways of dealing with problematic behaviors engage the parents as home therapists, enhancing the therapy. The parents become a therapeutic ally in the process of helping their child change and grow.

THERAPIST RESISTANCE

The child therapist must be able to endure unruly behavior, physical contact, and endless play that will be more pleasurable to the child than the adult. The therapist needs to be flexible enough to be able to play on the floor or in a sandbox with the child or to become messy with the child if the situation warrants it. She must also have the patience to deal with irate and/or defensive parents. However, the therapist who becomes totally involved in the relationship with the child becomes insulated from the day-to-day living experiences of the child within the family and other social contexts, and thus does not understand the child's contributions to disordered interpersonal functioning.

> An 8-year-old girl was being seen by a novice therapist who had been dealing with her as if the therapy session were a baby-sitting assignment. She tickled the child, at the child's request, rather than dealing with the meaning of the wish. Subsequent to that session, the child yelled, screamed, hit, spit, bit, and kicked the therapist while telling her that she was hated. The child's resistance to the therapist was not dealt with and the therapist attempted to assert her authority by restraining the child. Thus, we have the resistance of the child to her treatment and a counterresistance of the therapist to the child in response to the child's initial resistance.

There are other ways in which a therapist resists in therapy:

1. The therapist tries to be too understanding of aggressive fighting in a child who has been running roughshod over every limit and every person. The lack of limit setting creates great anxiety in the child who experiences the acceptance of the inappropriate behavior as lack of care and concern on the part of the therapist.

2. The therapist is too loving and understanding; the child experiences the therapist as seducing her to be loved in return. It is a false situation that the child is quick to detect and then proceeds to defeat the perceived unnatural sweetness of the adult by continuing to be a child no one can love. The child feels trapped and anxious, which is a stimulus for aggression.

3. The therapist refuses to set limits to action while allowing freedom of feeling. A failure to understand the constructive value of limits results in a failure to see and touch the living child behind the facade of resistance, defense, and developmental interferences.

Above all, the therapist needs to respect the children and treat them with dignity and understanding. These issues do not address all the ways in which therapists resist during the treatment of a child. Other problems will be dealt with in Chapter 8.

8

TRANSFERENCE AND COUNTERTRANSFERENCE

Transference and countertransference are two interrelated abstract concepts used to describe highly complex, interpersonal interactions in the therapeutic situation. In general, transference (or transference reaction) has been defined as the tendency to repeat in the present the past relationships with the significant people in one's childhood. A transference neurosis is a repetition within the therapeutic relationship of problematic patterns of functioning that have arisen from childhood relationships. Transference, transference reaction, and transference neurosis are well-documented phenomena in adult psychotherapy. The existence of these phenomena in child therapy has generated contradictory theorizing.

Countertransference is the process whereby the therapist repeats reactions and problems from her past in the therapeutic relationship with a patient. Countertransference also involves the personalized response of the therapist to the patient, based on the patient's need for the therapist to experience directly what the patient is experiencing. Thus, both transference and countertransference are experiences that arise from the therapeutic interaction. That these phenomena occur in child treatment has been debated.

TRANSFERENCE IN CHILD THERAPY

Panel discussions have addressed the issue of transference in child therapy. One group, headed by Joseph Sandler (Sandler et al. 1975) of the Hampstead Clinic in London, England, delineated four types of transference with children:

1. Habitual modes of relating: These are modes of relating to and attitudes toward the therapist that can be considered habitual and characteristic for the child with all adults. They are often seen in the earliest phases of treatment. Examples of habitual modes are developing angry provocative relationships, and pleasing the therapist. Habitual modes often serve as defenses against anxiety. Habitual modes may not be specific to the transference relationship but may involve a great deal of intense affect and action directed toward the therapist.

2. Current relationships: These are the displacements of current wishes, conflicts, and reactions onto the therapeutic situation, or onto the person of the therapist. They may be largely reality-related, for example, a sibling birth causes the child to display regressive behaviors. They can be a product of the developmental level of functioning expected at that age, for example, oedipal strivings in a 4-year-old. The important criterion here is the preoccupation of the child. How the child relates to real people in the present and the expression of that relationship in the therapeutic hour represent an extension or displacement from those present relationships. It is not considered a revival from the past as it is a current and ongoing behavioral expression within the present. An example of this is a current oedipal relationship with the parents displaced onto the therapeutic situation and the person of the therapist.

This is one of the difficulties in child therapy, that is, much of the material is active, ongoing, and external. The transference of current relationships is more likely to be seen in the prelatency child and in the early adolescent. These two groups share intense developmental reactions and conflicts that get played out within the therapeutic relationship.

3. Past experiences: Past experiences, wishes, fantasies, conflicts, and defenses are revived during therapy. They are a consequence of the development of therapy and now relate to the person of the therapist, both manifestly and symbolically. The transference here is a derivative of repressed material that emerges in relation to the person of the therapist, as a result of working through therapeutic issues. It combines present reality (including the therapist) with the expression of revived wishes, fantasies, and memories. What makes it difficult to distinguish from a present problem is the growing attachment of the child to the therapist. A current conflict might "spill over" into therapy, and appear as revived material because current conflicts are usually based on past patterns of behavior absorbed into subsequent developmental phases. It becomes confused at this point, and close contact with the home situation is very helpful.

4. Transference neurosis: This refers to the concentration of the child's conflicts, repressed infantile wishes, and fantasies on the person of the therapist, with the relative decrease of their manifestations outside therapy. As the child is in an active relationship with present-day love-objects, transference neurosis is much less evident. A. Freud (in Sandler et al. 1975) finds it convenient to think in terms of quantitative differences. A transference neurosis in a child is labeled when about three-quarters of the child's transference repetitions are within the therapeutic session, and

become much more diminished at home. Qualitatively speaking, it is necessary to look at the differences between real objects (parents) and fantasy objects that have been previously internalized. The process called transference neurosis with adults may occur for only very brief periods in child therapy. With adolescents, a full transference neurosis may not be possible because the adolescent is currently striving to break the ties with the parents, and conflicts are externalized by acting them out in relationships with others.

This conference concluded that there are transference manifestations and transferential involvement, but no real transference neurosis. The development of a transference neurosis requires the ability to contain an internal conflict that is a developmental task only gradually achieved.

The Hampstead group also studied special cases of transference such as in the borderline or psychotic child. The group has suggested that children who have experienced severe deprivations in their object relationships and/or in the capacity to make full object relationships (as a result, for example, of organicity or visual impairments) may use the therapist as an auxiliary ego. This may take the form of relating to the therapist as a real person or as a person able to satisfy a need.

Van Dam's (1967) discussion of transference in children focuses upon structures. He suggests that children must have reached some level of emotional maturity before transference phenomena will be expressed. He indicates that a transference neurosis needs the achievement of object constancy, ego autonomy, and a superego: object constancy allows an enduring working relationship to develop; ego autonomy permits the child to tolerate deprivation, reduce fear and impulsivity, and decrease motor discharge; and a superego provides the child with inner controls over behavioral manifestations of impulses. Berlin (1987) states, "Children have no other way of feeling about and of behaving with other adults than in the ways they have learned both to feel and behave toward their parents with largely unconsciously determined attitudes and feelings" (p. 101).

There are varying opinions about transference phenomena when treating children. That one obtains transference-like reactions from the child is not in doubt, but what to call it or how to categorize it is. We function on the premise that transference reaction in child treatment does occur and must be dealt with by the therapist. As in all other transactions, the cognitive and emotional levels of the child at the time must be taken into consideration.

TRANSFERENCE IN THE PRESCHOOL CHILD

In the preschool child transference phenomena are rare because the child is still dependent on mother and father, may not yet have achieved object constancy, is lacking in ego autonomy, and has not yet developed a superego. As Van Dam has suggested, without these structures in place a transfer to a new person is not possible. However, what does occur is an extension of the original behaviors, attitudes, and affects onto the meaningful relationship with the therapist (habitual mode of relating).

> Missy was 4 when originally seen in therapy due to extreme oppositional behavior. Her parents separated when she was 18 months and divorced when she was about 2 years of age. Not only did she experience a disruption in the loss of her father, but shortly thereafter she and her mother moved out of state.
>
> At the time of this therapy session, Missy was 5½. We had been sitting on the floor playing a swimming game when she abruptly got up, walked behind me, leaned over my shoulder, and slid down my body, giving the illusion she was coming through my legs. I commented upon her using my body as a slide, Missy smiled and continued the activity. The activity also had the symbolic equivalence of a birth phenomenon that I also commented upon after more repetitions. I

suggested that she was trying to find out how it would feel if she were born from my body. She repeated the activity three or four more times and then promptly walked out of the playroom down to the waiting room. I waited a few minutes for her return before I too went to the waiting room. She was sitting next to her mother's fiancé, her head in his lap, refusing to return to the playroom in spite of his encouragement. I suggested to both of them that we should stop for today and that I would see Missy next week. The following week as I arrived in the waiting room to pick her up, Missy seemed pleased to see me, then she looked angry, and finally she turned to her mother's fiancé who had again brought her and began flirting with him to his chagrin. Nevertheless, she readily came with me to the playroom. Once inside the room Missy asked me if I knew that her mother was going to college. When I replied positively she went on to say, "You know my mommy asked me whether she should go to school on Tuesday or Wednesday and I told her to go to school on Tuesday cause that's the day I see you. Do you know that my mommy calls you Sophie but I call you Dr. Lovinger cause that's a nicer name? Let's play Olympics."

Within the above two sessions, Missy expressed four basic issues:

1. her experienced desertion by her father (leaving the session),
2. her wish for another mother (telling her mother to take a class on the night she saw me),
3. oedipal issues (flirtation with mother's fiancé in the waiting room),
4. struggles to be competent (playing Olympics).

The issue of desertion for Missy was ongoing and present. Her leaving the session seemed a way of coping with the original narcissistic blow by being the actual doer (deserter) rather than the passive recipient (being deserted). This behavior pattern, that is, leaving the session, was a function of the therapy and was exhibited only within the therapeutic relationship. This was a midpoint in

Missy's working through the desertion she experienced and her attendant sense of badness.

Missy's wish for another mother and the oedipal issues expressed are both parts of the same process. With another mother there is safety in rejecting and/or competing with mother for the fiancé/daddy. However, it is also obvious, from the material presented, that Missy was also competing with me for the fiancé/daddy. This represents a transfer of feelings and behaviors of current relationships onto the therapist. The oedipal issues being dealt with by Missy are not a revival from the past. They are a current developmental issue in process of being solved.

TRANSFERENCE IN THE SCHOOL-AGE CHILD

Throughout this period, from about 6 to 12 years, the child exhibits increasing emotional and cognitive maturation, especially in terms of object constancy, ego autonomy, and superego development. Transference phenomena can range from the rarely seen, as in the preschool child, to a rather common occurrence, as in adult therapy.

> Eight-year-old Allison was referred by her mother because of hair pulling, resistance to parental demands, lying, and stealing. A diagnostic assessment of the child revealed an intact child who was struggling, reactively, against an overprotective mother who interfered with the child's increasing need for autonomy.
>
> In the early phase of treatment, Allison repeated with the therapist her relationship with her mother. The child was silent, did not ask for assistance, would rather do nothing than have to ask for something, and when setting up a game would push it toward the therapist, but would not ask the therapist to play in a direct, verbal manner.

With this child the transference phenomena were on two levels:

1. There was the clear extension of current relationship issues onto the therapeutic relationship expressed in Allison's doing everything by and for herself.
2. The nonverbal nature of the child's functioning within the therapy hour suggested that the issue was a revival of a past, similar issue stemming from a more nonverbal era.

During the school years, early transference phenomena can exist side by side with more mature transference elaborations.

In general, it is difficult to identify and use transference material in the treatment of children. The child's basic immaturity (as compared to more mature adult functioning), uneven mastery of basic drives, uneven development of ego functions, uneven superego development, and generalized egocentric functioning contribute to the limited capacity of children to develop full-fledged transferences, and to the child's resistance to the development of transference. This resistance often propels the child to use the therapist as a new experience, for example, tolerating freedom of thoughts, actions, and fantasy, and helping against anxiety. A review of the literature on child treatment did not turn up articles addressing the result of the child responding to an adult who does not react to her in an expectable manner. The usual judgmental, cultural responses are missing in the communicative process between therapist and child. This different responsiveness is both a challenge to the development of a transference and an interpretation, even if a nonspecific one.

Transference Interpretation

There are four basic principles delineated for the interpretation of transference phenomena:

1. Don't interpret at the beginning of therapy as it can cause strong resistance to the process of therapy.
2. Interpret when there is a substantial or growing resistance.

3. Interpret when transference phenomena are intense or at an optimal level.
4. Interpret when understanding can be obtained.

But caution must be used. Analyzing transference phenomena in children and providing insight into dynamics and etiology interferes with the natural maturational processes within the child and places upon the child expectations of adult behavior and understandings. Spiegel (1989) states,

> It is important that in working with children, the emphasis be on the exposition and clarification of feelings and the rectification of disoriented feelings. However, it is not only erroneous, it is a serious error to try to provide the youngster with any understanding of transference and of the dynamics and etiology of his disorder. [p. 198]

COUNTERTRANSFERENCE

Countertransference was defined by Fenichel (1945) as an unconsciously determined attitudinal set held by the therapist that interferes with her work. The cure for countertransference was more analysis for the therapist. Although Annie Reich (1960) eloquently described the countertransference process as a spontaneous insight or gestalt into the patient's problem via the analyst's own unconscious, this position was not readily accepted. She spoke of countertransference as a partial and necessarily short-lived identification with the patient. The therapist then must be able to swing back to an outside position, to objectively evaluate what was just felt from within. Thus, countertransference was considered a tool for understanding and listening to the unconscious of the client via freefloating attention or by becoming the participant observer. Reich concludes that "countertransference is a necessary prerequisite of analysis. If it does not exist, the necessary talent and interest are lack-

ing. But it has to remain shadowy and in the background" (p. 282).
Berlin (1987) states,

> Analysts have long known that their emotional reactions comprise
> a most important tool and a potential insidious hazard. They can
> help the analyst understand his patients through delicate empathy
> or perception of his own responses to the patient's intentions, or
> they can produce perilous blind spots and evoke anti-therapeutic
> behaviour. It is unfortunate that many gather the complex array of
> such emotions under the single umbrella of countertransference and
> thus blur the distinctions between them. Indeed, the term has
> become a cliché which enables the user to label his behavior without
> examining its exact nature. [p. 105]

Countertransference as a phenomenon in adult therapy is generally accepted. However, countertransference in child therapy is not
often discussed in the literature. Marshall (1979) suggests that overwhelming feelings of guilt, inadequacy and anxiety may be at the root
of the neglect of countertransference as it relates to children. Waksman
(1986) and Norman (1989) suggest that the countertransference
stresses on the child therapist are more severe than on the adult therapist. This is related to the unconscious conflict of the therapist with
the child's parents as well as the nature of the child's material.

The conflict with the parents can be related to:

1. identification with the child against the parent,
2. identification with the parent against the child,
3. a protective attitude to the child against the world,
4. a therapist who is over critical of parents, which leads to
   difficulty in understanding the child's normal healthy de-
   pendence on parents as well as the infantile elements due
   to conflicts.

The nature of the child's material can limit the therapist's
effectiveness in dealing with countertransference reactions. This
material can include:

1. highly charged affects,
2. unpredictability of behavior,
3. egocentricity of thinking and closeness of productions to the unconscious,
4. seductiveness and provocativeness of behavior,
5. symbolically obscured nature of communication,
6. intensity of both positive and negative feelings.

The two basic countertransference reactions to this material are (1) destructive thoughts, impulses, and feelings toward child clients; and (2) sexual feelings toward the child. Marshall (1979) has attempted to organize and elaborate four types of countertransference reactions encountered in child therapy:

1. The unconscious, therapist-derived response (type I) is the most difficult type of countertransference, requiring additional treatment for the therapist as it arises from the problems of the therapist. However, the biggest problem is identifying it since it remains in the unconscious and the therapist is unaware of its existence. Recognition signs applicable to children and adolescents include:

   a. excessive play with diminution of talk;
   b. quick yielding to requests;
   c. gratification of the child, particularly feeding and gift giving;
   d. any strong feeling especially accompanied by guilt or anxiety;
   e. lulling, which alters attention, and the child plays out similar fantasies repetitively;
   f. impulsive talk or action;
   g. physical contact;
   h. allowing parents to use the child's time;
   i. consultation with parents or others without the child's involvement or agreement;

  j.   strong, unresolved feelings toward parents;
  k.   inability to involve parents appropriately;
  l.   preoccupation with changing behavior especially as
       desired by parents or school (Marshall 1979).

   Personal psychoanalysis or analytic supervision is recommended to resolve countertransference problems (Marshall
1979). Additionally, Friend suggests analyzing the infan-
tile-parental conflicts of the therapist. This includes both
the need to maintain a nurturing, feminine identity, and
the need to maintain a powerful, masculine identity. Unconscious, seductive, erotic desires, desires for leadership
and omnipotence, and the therapist's own narcissistic needs
are grist for the therapeutic mill to resolve countertrans-
ferential reactions (Friend 1972).
2. Type II countertransference reactions are like type I in that
   both are therapist generated. However, these reactions are
   conscious. The therapist is aware of the problem but does
   not know how to resolve it. Good supervision should be
   of help in this situation.
3. Type III countertransference stagnates or slows the therapy.
   Marshall indicated that although much may seem to go on
   in the session, no real movement occurs because the child
   is in control of the treatment. Perhaps type III reactions
   can be more easily seen as a the resistance to therapy. Supervision of any kind is deemed helpful to move type III to
   type IV countertransference.
4. Type IV countertransference defines the child's responsibility for inducing thoughts and feelings (but not actions)
   in the therapist that are within the therapist's awareness.
   The therapist's most important task is to understand the
   communication of the countertransference by studying the
   interactional field, tracing the source of the countertrans-
   ferential reactions, and devising appropriate interventions.

Norman (1989) has suggested two types of traps for the therapist of children. These are:

1. The analyst is often hampered in his ability to be aware of what is going on inside himself.
2. At the same time the child is bombarding the analyst with urgent demands. The material presented by the child can reach beyond the analyst's defenses and actualize those infantile phase-specific problems and feelings that were left behind in development and never integrated. [p. 117]

Norman further states that the emotional turmoil experienced in a session with a child is similar to the visual images and fantasies one develops in a session with an adult patient. However, the therapist responds with feelings just as the child talks directly to the therapist's experience of her own childhood.

In one session with 11-year-old Teddy, the therapist was particularly frustrated with Teddy's repeated alteration of the rules of the game being played whenever it looked as if Teddy would lose. She could not follow his changes and play the game as he was then suggesting. Finally, in frustration she pushed her chair back, crossed her arms in front of her, and said, "If you're not going to play by the rules, I won't play with you anymore." The child gave her a surprised look and in her head she said, "What have you done?" The therapist was able to recognize her feelings—she felt like an 11-year-old at that moment.

In child therapy, the immediate demands of the child violate the therapist's space and interfere with the therapist's ability to introspect before responding. Thus, there may be more countertransference reactions in child treatment than adult.

Countertransference (Marshall's type IV) can be a powerful and indeed essential tool in psychotherapeutic work. With the anxiety, guilt, and fear of the constant and strong regressive pull in work with children and adolescents, what we fear most provides the potential for the most movement and therapeutic gain. As a therapist is able to master his own fears, and illuminate the darkest corners of the soul, so too can the courage and hope necessary for such a voyage be shared with the patient, and its seed planted to grow. Both transference and countertransference are inseparable parts of the therapeutic relationship. No one theory or approach can encompass all the forms encountered in therapy. At best we can continue to struggle with and work through the countertransference and understand ourselves and the children with whom we work.

9

DREAMS

Dreams have long been considered messages to be understood, interpreted, and responded to depending on the culture and needs of the society. Freud (1900) saw dreams as "the royal road to the unconscious" and used them extensively in his developing treatment modality. While there are a number of theories of dreams, dream interpretation that is usable with children has been haphazard at best. Rather, Freud's approach to and his understanding of adult dreams has been applied, with little modification to children's dreams. Foulkes (1982, 1990), using children's dreams from various levels of development, suggests that the translation of dream theory from adult to child obscures our understanding of the productions of children.

Foulkes suggests that dreams are products of our knowledge of ourselves and our understanding of the world and reflect the organization of our cognitive development at any given point in time. Their development follows waking cognitive growth. Dreams cannot directly reflect what we see or what we do, but they can express our knowledge of these things. A knowledge base and cognitive skills are necessary precursors allowing us to recombine memories and knowledge into dreams.

Ekstein (1981) has suggested that children's dreams could be considered as a fairy tale:

> Behind every tale there is a bit of psychological truth. The fairy tale is not only magic wish fulfillment, the happy ending, but it is also the representation of inner conflict, of developmental tasks and developmental dilemmas. The fairy tale is more than a cautionary tale. It is not only a warning but also an attempt at solution. Behind the happy ending there is hidden, it seems to me, an adaptive solution. [p. 122]

Both Foulkes and Ekstein suggest that dreams at different ages and levels of development reflect the issues and struggles with which the child is dealing. Unlike Freud, Ekstein suggests that play rather than dreams is the royal road to the unconscious of the child and that there are many similarities between dreaming and playing.

DREAMS OF PRESCHOOLERS

Dreams during this period of development are usually only a sentence or two long, taking place at home or in an outdoor setting, although the settings are usually vague and undefined. The characters of the dreams typically include representations of the self and sometimes family members or familiar adults. However, the dreams of children at this age do not include unknown adults. While human figures are sometimes present, animals are the predominant figures in young children's dreams as in this following dream told by a 3-year-old: "Animals were walking down the street." These animals are domesticated and/or familiar species (e.g., dogs, horses, pigs, chickens, lions, tigers, deer, monkeys).

Themes of dreams are related to body functions of thirst, hunger, and sleep, and unfold in an episodic manner with no real organization. Feeling states related to developmental level are not represented in dream sequences, nor are issues of autonomy, greater differentiation, and identification. They are expressed as sleep difficulties such as problems in falling asleep, night walking, fears of ghosts and wild animals, the inability to sleep alone, desire to sleep with parents, and rituals at bedtime. These sleep disturbances are the symptoms of the difficulty rather than the difficulty itself.

A study by Beaudet (1990) who collected a series of dreams from four preschoolers, demonstrated that looking at dreams over a span of time often revealed the child's working through of the dilemma he posited within the first dream. The dreams of the three boys in the study reflected much anxiety around issues that were focused within the home, while the dreams of the one girl reflected anxiety around issues relating to the wider world. This finding parallels the work of Erikson (1950), who suggested that boys were directed toward the wider world and hence would experience more anxiety when dealing with issues within the narrower world of the family, and girls were more interested in the narrower world of the family and hence would experience more anxiety in the wider world. As Foulkes suggested, the dreams of the children were only a sentence or two. However, verbal elaboration of the dream material, in conjunction with drawings, led to highly detailed explorations and expansions of the dream.

DREAMS OF SCHOOL-AGE CHILDREN

There are different emotional and cognitive issues dealt with in these children's dreams.

Five to Seven

Dream reports at this age double in length, are sequential in that they tell a simple story, are more dynamic, express social interaction between the people in the dream, and portray the dreamer as an observer. Dreams are commonly set at home or in recreational environments where play activities predominate. The activities are initiated by characters other than the dreamer. The actors in the dream, as during the preschool years, are nuclear family members and other known people. While animals are still present, there is a decrease in the amount they are represented. Strangers, for the first time, are now present in dreams. The young child, up to about 5 or 6 may confuse dreams with waking fantasies and may report a dream as an actual event. There still do not appear to be affective states as in the following dream of a 5½-year-old girl:

> Sara describes herself as lying on her bed asleep in her dream. In the dream she awakens and notices green smoke filling the room. She discovers, at the same time, she is lying on the bed with hands and feet tied to the corners. She is gagged.

Dreams during these ages are like simple slices of life, but with no fully elaborated fantasies. Foulkes's research suggests that speculation ran against the grain in this age group. Children, because of their level of cognitive development, tried to concretely grasp a phenomenon, but could not theorize. Children of this age group begin to construct a world in their dreams that is modeled on the real one in which characters performed activities, pursued goals, and realized the consequences of their action as in this second dream of Sara's.

> A girl whose name was also Sara, but was not her, bought a china doll against the wishes of another girl and the storekeeper. The girl named Sara keeps the china doll locked in her closet at night. One night, the china doll uses her fingernail to break the lock, escape from the closet, and kill the girl.

Sleep disturbances during this period of development begin to look like the sleep disturbances of adults. Rituals may be needed by the child before going to bed. These often include getting a glass of water, going to the bathroom, being tucked in and kissed, closing the curtains in a particular way, and so on. Nightmares, night terrors, and somnambulism can occur, but the rituals are the most distinctive feature at this age.

Seven to Nine

By this level of development dreams have changed once again. They have gained markedly in formal organization which allows subjects to be played against each other. The dream plots themselves contain scenarios reflecting clear narrative intentions as well as enduring childhood concerns. These concerns seem to motivate the dreamer to organize the dream content in complex and personally meaningful ways. The dreams themselves reflect the developmental task of the era, for example the wish to be a competent boy or girl. In addition, the self character within the dream is a thinking and feeling person. The dreams are more complex and depict a variety of activities, feeling states, characters, and settings.

> Seven-year-old Tommy reported a "nightmare" during a therapy session. He got up one morning and wiped his mouth with his hand and six teeth fell out, which he promptly lost so he couldn't put them under his pillow for the tooth fairy. He was hungry and no one else was up so he went downstairs to the kitchen. He fixed some cornflakes and milk and in his first spoonful of milk were the six teeth.

Nine to Twelve

There do not seem to be qualitative changes in dreams during this age group from the previous one. Rather, the formal powers of dream organization are well consolidated. There is much sex-role stereotyping and, concurrent with this, personality differences become prominent.

Ten-year-old Dale related a dream with increasing excitement. He
was playing baseball and was up at bat. Brushing off the plate resulted
in finding some pennies. As he brushed more and deeper he found
nickels. The deeper he brushed, the larger the coin he found.

Eleven-year-old Joel went fishing in his dream with his father. He
caught a fish that automatically flew into the freezer, which had
four levels. He looked at his fish later and found rats, ten in each of
three levels. He kept one rat for a pet and scared his older sister
with it.

Over the course of childhood dreams become increasingly
complex as can be seen in the dreams above. One must conclude,
therefore, that dream making is subject to the same developmental
patterning as are waking cognitive skills. This does not mean that
there are no meanings in children's dreams, but rather that they
reflect current waking development, are a rehearsal for developmental roles, and express current developmental dilemmas and
concerns.

Twelve-year-old Jason, just on the brink of puberty, said he had
had a dream that he was the only boy on a girl's baseball team. In
the dream he hit a home run and all the girls came over to him,
patted him on the back, and told him what a wonderful job he had
done. Then they all went to the locker room to shower. When
asked what happened next he commented that he woke up.

DREAMS OF LATE
SCHOOL-AGE (9–11) CHILDREN

Foulkes found these years to be a time of quantitative growth, such
as in the length of dreams or the frequency of remembering, rather
than qualitative change. Personality differences began to surface in
dream content, which he thought was due to successful acquisition
of skills in dreaming. He proposes that the ability to reflect indi-

vidual personality in dreams is only possible after the imperatives of cognitive development have been met.

More dynamically, Mack (1965) reported that under the age of 2, threatening personality aspects of people are seen as menacing machines, noises, or animals. Between the ages of 2 to 5, biting animals and simple monsters inhabit the child's dream. No differentiation between the sexes occurs if people are present in the dream. After 5, more sophisticated monsters and human figures are differentiated as far as sex. However, he stresses that due to the regressive forces at work, percepts in dreams can be characteristic of earlier developmental levels and can appear along with later developmental levels. Because children and adults often have conflicts and anxieties about destructive figures in dreams, the content is often related to early parental relationships. The largest number of dreams express wishes or fears. Unpleasant dreams are more common than pleasant ones. Unpleasant dreams usually consist of the contents of personal physical injury, falling, being chased or kidnapped, fires, and supernatural creatures. The themes of pleasant dreams can involve finding, acquiring, or receiving toys, food, clothes, money, and pets; amusements; travel; and play. In terms of general dream content, parents are the most frequent topic and are usually in a pleasant role. Animals with a definite fear element are the second most common and include lions, tigers, bears, apes, and snakes.

NIGHTMARES

In discussing nightmares, Mack (1965) feels that it is "intense anxiety of overwhelming proportions, the sense of danger and helplessness, and the occurrence or threat of violent attack, directed especially at the dreamer" (p. 412). Mack notes that there are two divisions of nightmares. The first is the rapid eye movement (REM) sleep phase nightmare, or severe anxiety dream. The mental content of the dream itself tends to be persecutory, violent toward the dreamer, and sometimes very elaborate. Fear is the main affect; however, the awakened dreamer can be calmed, and is usually coherent, oriented, and not hallucinating. There is no perspiration, and the incident can be remembered, along with the content of the dream. The second type, the non-REM nightmare, or night terror, involves greater signs of physical involvement. The night terror occurs during the sleep or in a twilight state between sleeping and waking. The child may sit up in bed, jump to the floor, run about the room, or scream out. Overwhelming terror is the result, while the mental state is confused. The child cannot be readily calmed and cannot recognize objects. He may continue to have the dream even after being awakened, as if he is hallucinating. He may perspire heavily, and there is complete amnesia for the event and the dream.

The child must learn to differentiate between an action and a thought or be faced with parental disappointment, which may be translated by the child into abandonment, loss of nurturance and love, or annihilation through parental retaliation. The child's first nightmares, then, are often a result of these struggles with aggression coming not only from himself but from others. The fear of retaliation for one's feelings evokes different reactions at different ages. Early in the second year of life, the loss of the love object can mean loss of food, warmth, affection, and protection. Around the age of 2 to 3, the fear is of the other person retaliating and thus losing the love available.

In presenting a theory of nightmares, Mack (1965) notes that there are some similarities to dreams. He feels that anxiety over present conflicts gets tied up with past conflicts. This results in a regression to an earlier developmental level within the dream, stirring up early fears and wishes along the way. It is not only these old fears that are revived but also the ego state that went along with those fears. The defenses of intellectualization and repression are not available. Ego functions that help the dreamer evaluate dangerous situations and distinguish frightening thoughts from frightening situations are also weakened. Also, due to the lack of object ties, significant others are not available to help the child in reality testing. Because of this, all perceptions within the dream are treated as if they were external to the dreamer and real. When so much anxiety is triggered by such a frightening possibility, the only recourse is to wake up. After a nightmare, small children often require reunion with the parents in order to reestablish evaluative capabilities, unlike the adult who can usually depend on his own ego functions.

Dreams appear to serve a multitude of purposes, as do fantasies. Among these are tension reduction, problem solving, an outlet for creativity, and a way to preserve sleep.

USING DREAMS IN THERAPY

Children seldom report their dreams spontaneously. Occasionally when a younger child is asked to tell a dream he will relate a fantasy that he has had but that he believes he dreamed. It is a common practice for a child to add to the dream or modify it so it makes sense to him. Children also often respond to direct questions about their dreams by saying, "I forgot," "I don't know," "I don't dream." However, during a play session a child will more readily discuss his dreams through a doll, some other toy, or drawings.

In a different approach, Anna Freud (1965b) treats the dream content very much as she would dream content in adults. Yet Melanie Klein (1975) indicates that the approach in child analysis must be different from that of the analysis of adults. She also points out that there is a close relationship between dreams, daydreams, and fantasies in the play activities of children. In fact she states that children often express in play the same thing that they tell in dreams. Although Klein used dreams in her treatment of children, she saw play as "the most important medium of expression." In fact, the interpretation of a child's dreams endangers the therapy. It becomes apparent to the child that dreams reveal secrets they do not wish anyone to guess at, thus causing the child to "shut down" not only in relating dreams but in all other areas of functioning as well. The dream material, however, is not ignored but used by the therapist as the therapy progresses.

In child therapy, it is immaterial whether the dream is at night or during the day, a fantasy or just an elaboration. All aspects of the communication can be used in the service of resolving conflicts and difficulties in living. The additions the child creates could be considered associations to the material being presented and hence will clarify the communication. Since focusing upon dream material often results in the child's resistance to reporting this material, I ask children to draw their dreams. We can then talk about the drawings, gain elaborations and clarifications of the parts of the dream, as well as hear the feeling tones embedded in the dream. Careful reflection of the feelings and dilemmas, with measured response to the child's reaction to my interventions, is as far as I take the working through of the dream communication.

10

TERMINATION

When to end treatment is an issue that did not receive a great deal of attention in the adult literature until the 1950s. There is even less attention to this issue in the child literature. This problem is complicated by the knowledge that approximately 72 percent of analyses end prematurely, that is, without mutuality of agreement that treatment has accomplished all that can be done. Novick (1982) has suggested that the premature termination seen in adult treatment represents a regression to adolescent enactments of the avoidance of last issues rather than resolution of them. Clearly, in treatment with children, adolescent-level functioning will not be achieved. Thus, termination with children must use other criteria.

A. Freud (1970) suggested that once children have resumed normal development, treatment can be considered at an end. This is a position I use in my work with children with one further consideration. Since much of development progresses toward greater separation, individuation, and differentiation, peer involvement becomes an important area of support for the developing child. Therefore, the child, in addition to resuming development, should

also be more involved with peer activities and should be developing adequate peer relationships.

It is difficult to say goodbye to a person one has been in intimate contact with over a period of time, especially when an ongoing relationship is not going to continue. Attachments have been
created that need to be dealt with tactfully and sensitively. This is
often not the case in the lives of children, as can be seen in the year-
end school promotions. Goodbyes are often perfunctory and minimal. Children do not have a chance to work out their feelings about
the loss of an important person in their lives, one they have lived
with for a year. That is unfortunate. Treatment should have a better ending, even when the treatment is not completed. This chapter discusses various forms of the termination process for the child,
the parent, and the therapist.

CHILD TERMINATION

There are times when a child, after a period of time in treatment,
decides she no longer wants to come, for reasons such as the lack of
time to play with friends and toys and to watch television. Clearly,
one to five hours a week do not represent a real loss of time for
these activities. However, erupting issues that are too painful to look
at or deal with are the most likely motivation to avoid the treatment. How can a therapist deal with this situation? Interpretation
of the resistance may help in some instances. My experience has
led me to conclude that the most helpful way of dealing with the
resistance to treatment on the level of termination is to let the child
go. Of course, parents need to be apprised of your assessment of
what is happening and given help and support to deal with their
child's autonomous decision.

> Nine-year-old Grace decided she did not want to come to treatment
> any more after about 4 months of weekly sessions. In fact, she took

half an hour to reach the playroom from the waiting room while walking at a snail's pace. When she seemed to be arriving at the door too quickly she moved back toward the waiting room. When she finally came into the playroom she would not utter a word and sat in stony silence for the remainder of the session. The following day her mother called stating that the child absolutely refused to return. She was distraught about the child's behavior and asked what could be done. I suggested she see me the following week.

In session with the mother she commented that her husband did not see any reason for the child to continue treatment as there had been decided changes in the child's behavior. The father's resistance seemed more related to his lack of understanding of the mother's concern and of the child's real problems. Mother felt that Grace needed more work. I told the mother that keeping the child in treatment with such massive resistance would be counterproductive and might work to the detriment of the child. Rather, we should allow the child to make this decision with some limits. Mother would agree with Grace not returning to see me as long as the changes in her behavior continued. Further, the mother expected specific functioning from her. As long as Grace could continue to adhere to these limitations, the mother would not insist on her returning to see me. However, if Grace were to relapse, then back into treatment she would go. While the mother was still unhappy with this decision she could understand that the approach I was proposing was in the current best interests of the child. I did not hear from this family again.

Ten-year-old Lenny brought his mother into a session so he could tell me he did not want to come back and see me because he was very angry with me. He was unable to tell me what was making him so angry. As the discussion continued, his anger grew until he hit out at me with his fist and ran out of the room. His mother was as perplexed as I was about the motivation for all the negative feelings Lenny was expressing. I suggested to the mother she not insist he come back to see me, as the intensity of the child's feelings would interfere with the treatment. She, too, was quite disappointed in the outcome, but was willing to respond to her child's wishes. Some two years later I received a call from this family requesting services again. This time Lenny had asked to come back to see me. As Lenny and I discussed what had happened previously he was able to tell me that he did not want to hear what I told him about his feelings, especially since I was right. As we continued to work, his reaction to my poorly timed interpretation was worked through over and again.

There are many reasons why a child will refuse treatment and the refusal can seem implacable, making treatment untenable. Allowing the child to leave may pave the way for the child to return at a later time when she can make better use of the treatment. This approach, at the end of treatment, follows through on the approach at the beginning of treatment, that is, treating the child with respect and dignity.

PARENT TERMINATION

Parents terminate the treatment of their children for a wide variety of reasons: lack of understanding of the process of treatment, both positive and negative changes in the child's behavior, lack of commitment to treatment, and increasing cost and the financial stress on the family. While it is easy to attribute these factors to resistance, with its implied reluctance or inability to tolerate the changes, in the child there can also be reality factors that must be considered and handled by the therapist, sensitively and tactfully.

As was discussed in an earlier chapter, from my first meeting with parents I work at engaging them in the process of treatment. I explain the process and the reasons I believe that treatment will take a period of time longer than 10 sessions. *Consumer Reports* (1995) discusses the positive outcomes that accrue from longer treatment periods. The Division of Psychotherapy of the American Psychological Association (Rubinstein et al. 1991) has published a helpful brochure entitled "Psychotherapy with Children and Adolescents: A Guide for Parents." Using these materials may be helpful, but even more helpful is the availability of the therapist, especially when crises occur. I specifically inform parents that when issues arise in the treatment of their children that might cause disruptions in the family, I will help them manage the situations that might arise from them. I will also schedule conferences, with the child's permission, to help parents deal with ongoing issues as well. I have found that when parents are made an integral part of the therapeutic endeavor, resistance to or premature terminations are rare. The resistance attributed to time commitments necessary for treatment are also circumvented by the processes I have just described.

Financial considerations are real and present problems for our patients and their families. The family can be referred to a clinic with sliding fees. However, once I have established a relationship with a child and her family, I feel a commitment to them and the therapeutic process. I will reduce my fee to allow the therapy to continue where I know that the family's circumstances make this a necessity. The parents and I work out issues of the fee reduction and the possible shame and guilt that may be attendant, along with any other issues that might arise as a result of this alteration.

Novick (1990) comments that there are times parents are reluctant to have the treatment of their children end. While this does not happen often, when it does occur the parents need a period of time to work through their separation.

> Fourteen-year-old Bill, a closed-head–injured child requested that he be finished with treatment by the time he entered junior high school. This request had been made for some one to two years before he was due to change schools. (He entered school late because of his immaturity and he lost a year due to the post-trauma hospitalization.) He could not clearly articulate why he needed treatment to end but it was clearly an important goal for him. Mother was quite resistant to this idea. She verbalized fears that Bill would lose whatever gains he had made when seeing me or that I would not

see Bill or have time for him if he left treatment. Mother and I had periodic contact during the last year of Bill's treatment to help her deal with the issues she raised and the underlying fears they tapped. Toward the end of Bill's last year in grade school she reluctantly agreed to the termination. I did arrange with both the mother and Bill that I would see him six months after we stopped to reassess the situation for both of them. Bill was accepting of this arrangement and his mother seemed soothed. Both were quite pleased when I next saw them. Bill's therapeutic gains had been maintained and the mother was reassured.

The working-through process with the mother was critically important to a good termination process.

THERAPIST TERMINATION

Termination with children differs from termination in adult treatment for a number of reasons:

1. Children's basic development is not complete. In adults there is growth and development but at a different pace. Some issues in children can only be dealt with temporarily because of cognitive and emotional limits.
2. Children do not understand the necessity to deal with the feelings generated by the goodbye process.
3. Children's treatment is not really complete when termination occurs because of ongoing development.

The younger the child the more difficult it is for her to understand what termination is about.

Her therapist talked with 5-year-old Julie about her worries having gone away and how much better she had been feeling. The child agreed to this, but when the therapist suggested she might not need to come see her anymore Julie turned her back and proceeded to ignore her. This behavior was repeated week after week with Julie sometimes querying why the therapist was telling her this. When the therapist explained that she would still be in her office but that Julie would not be coming, the child's behavior and understanding shifted and she was able to talk about the ending of treatment. Julie responded to the therapist as if the therapist were saying she was going to die. When Julie was reassured this was not the case, she could deal with termination and the issues associated with saying good-bye.

Therapist termination occurs in two basic ways: (1) when the child begins to sum up the treatment history, and (2) when the therapist becomes aware of the resolution of issues that initiated the treatment and the resumption of normal development.

The child who is summing up typically contrasts how she was when first entering treatment and how she is now. In a wide sense the child is describing her inner journey while at the same time narrating the history of the experiential therapeutic relationship. For me this is a sad time, just as saying good-bye to people I have developed relationships with over time engenders sadness. During this phase of termination I listen to the story the child evolves, adding pieces that may have been "forgotten." Well into this process of summing up I suggest that maybe the child no longer needs to talk with me about her worries. I typically assess how the child responds to this suggestion in subsequent sessions and then the child and I set an ending date, one that is consonant with a typical break in the treatment, such as vacation time.

> Ten-year-old Jonathan spent some months summing up his treatment when I finally broached termination. He seemed comfortable with ending treatment and a date corresponding with the winter holidays was mutually set. However, as our ending date approached he told me that he was going to keep coming because he had been having nightmares he needed to talk about, but then

proceeded to tell me he could not remember what these nightmares were.

I heard this communication as the child's need for more time to
deal with issues of loss (his parents had recently divorced and his
father had moved out of town). We continued to process his feelings about the divorce and the loss of his father in his day-to-day
living situation. When summer vacation arrived he was more settled
about the ending of treatment and his relationship with me.

While children review their treatment as they move close to
termination, the more usual way children deal with endings is
expressed in their greater interest in activities with peers and other
events. Invitations to join in activities and the development of peer
relationships give us the clearest picture of the emotional growth
of the child as well as the resolution of those difficulties that have
interfered with age-appropriate functioning. Presentation of ending treatment is recognized by the child as the next step. The child
can then be helped to review the treatment and assess where she
was as compared with where she is now. The summing up is an
important part of the ending of treatment.

The treatment of any person is never completed. There is work
that is done over the years after treatment formally ends. This is
especially so for children whose cognitive, emotional, and maturational growth has not completed enough to fully resolve many of
the issues that initiated treatment.

> I first saw Alexa when she was 8. Her compulsive rituals, which had
> begun in a circumscribed area of functioning, were now spreading to
> most areas of her life. After about a year of treatment she was able to
> recognize that her rituals were an attempt to prevent her mother
> from dying. Her rituals disappeared and her functioning improved
> dramatically after this understanding. However, her underlying separ-
> ation issues related to her mother could not be dealt with in any fullness
> because of her age. Nevertheless, she was developing relationships
> with peers and functioning adequately in other areas of her life. Issues

of termination arose and were resolved and the child left treatment. She did return to treatment during her college years to deal again with the issue of separation from her mother.

Because of the immaturity of the child some major life problems cannot be fully dealt with and must wait for greater cognitive and emotional growth before resolution can occur. At termination our work is incomplete and must wait for the further development of our child clients.

Appendix A: Intake Interview

In this appendix and the one that follows, I formally present information for assessments of the family's needs. Appendix A deals with the intake interview and the issues of the family context of the child in developmental distress, family interactions, family understanding of the child, and other contributions to the child's dysfunctional behavior. Appendix B provides the reader with a format for organizing the data generated by psychological assessments. This data can help focus treatment and alerts the clinician to problems and conflicts not readily available through interviews at the beginning of treatment.

IDENTIFYING DATA

Don is a 10-year-old Caucasian boy who is currently in the fifth grade. He is good looking, with light brown hair and a fair complexion. His height and weight are average for his age (approximately 4'10" and 95 pounds). At home he lives with his father and mother, two brothers (Tim, 17 years, and Danny, 7 years), and one sister (Nancy, 13 years). Don was referred for psychological evaluation at the request of his parents; Mrs. G. said that they wanted to know if he had a "learning disability." They didn't know what constituted a learning disability but knew that he was having difficulty in school, especially with math, English, and spelling. When asked why they came to the center, Mrs. G. said that Dr. F. (an ophthalmologist) recommended it. In 1970 Dr. D. diagnosed Don as needing glasses. It was at this time that Don was having a great deal of difficulty with reversal of letters in reading. The glasses were worn for two years and the reversal trend slowly diminished. In October he was reexamined and diagnosed as having an astigmatism. In November Mrs. G. took Don to Dr. F. "to get another opinion about Don's vision." Dr. F. said that Don had no visual acuity impairment and that he did not need glasses. Don stopped wearing glasses at that time. Dr. F. examined Don in April and September of the following year and found nothing to change his original diagnosis. The next January, Mrs. G. again called Dr. F. because Don was doing poorly in school and seemed to be having reading problems. Dr. F. then recommended that he come to the center for "psychometric testing" because he is not "interpreting" what he sees.

INFORMANTS

Mr. and Mrs. G. arrived early for their appointment. They were neatly attired in what appeared to be their everyday clothes and were quietly waiting in the reception area. During the interview it was Mrs. G. who gave most of the information. Only on one occasion did Mr. G. add anything and then it was usually after Mrs. G. could not answer or wanted confirmation of her answer.

Both were cooperative and gave information when asked specific questions but rarely volunteered anything beyond the scope of the question. The one exception to this was where Don's schoolwork was concerned. Mrs. G. gladly expounded on all she knew about that topic. They seemed to be genuinely concerned about Don's difficulties and were willing to do what they could to help.

HOME ENVIRONMENT

Don lives with his parents, two brothers, and sister in a private home. Situated as they are, out in the country, they have no close neighbors. Once in a while, Don will have a friend over but usually plays by himself or with his younger brother. While his older brother and sister have their own bedrooms, Don shares a room and a double bed with Danny. He says that he doesn't mind and that they get along okay together.

The family does not usually go out and do things together on a regular basis. They do, however, take an occasional trip together and like to go camping in the summertime. At home playing cards seems to be one of the more popular pastimes and one that Don really enjoys. He and Danny also play other games together.

DEVELOPMENT

Don was a planned full-term baby who weighed approximately seven pounds at birth. The mother had a normal labor but had to have a cesarean section performed because the afterbirth was beginning to break up. She encountered no further difficulties and recovered well from the operation. Don was "wide eyed" and healthy at birth. He has maintained his health well since that time with the exception of a bout with the measles (no abnormally high temperature) and just recently a touch of tonsillitis. However, this latest problem cleared up and no further difficulty has been experienced.

Mrs. G. stated that Don had no major problems in being weaned, at approximately 1½ years, or with toilet training at approximately 2 years of age. He displayed no difficulties with walking, talking, or any other stages of his development to date. Both Don and his mother indicated that he has no problems sleeping, although he did wake up once several weeks ago because of a nightmare. When asked, he said that he couldn't remember experiencing it but did relate two other dreams that he did remember. The nightmare, as told by his mother, was about one of his teachers, and Don woke up crying, saying, "She's going to get me, she's going to get me." After 10 to 15 minutes he calmed down and went back to sleep. He has not reported any further episodes of this particular dream.

SCHOOL ENVIRONMENT

Don attends a small country school run by the Catholic Church. He is in the fifth grade along with five other boys and ten girls. During some of their classes they share a room with the fourth grade. He has two teachers. Both are women in their mid-fifties. Sister R., who is also the principal, teaches English, science, social studies, geography, history, and religion. Mrs. B., a lay person, teaches math and spelling. Although Don says that Mrs. B. is his favorite, it was she who was in his recent nightmare. Mrs. G. said that she would have expected it to be Sister R., as she had never seen her smile and she is very strict.

Don had been attending this parochial school since the first grade. Although his mother says that he is having more difficulty in the fifth grade than he had in the fourth, his grades did not confirm this viewpoint. Since the third grade, there have been no major changes in his grades, with the exception of math which went from a C to a D. In general his grades run in the C range with an occasional B (art) and/or D (math). One of the problems, as related by both teachers, is that Don never asks for help. His peers find it difficult to accept his weaknesses and are now saying things like "that dummy G." He has one fairly close buddy at school, a boy who also exhibits some learning problems.

Although Don said that he likes school, his mother indicated that he does not like school as much this year and has frequently expressed the desire to attend public school. His teachers told me that he is not a behavior problem and usually sits quietly until called upon. At times, "You hardly know that he's there." Both teachers said that he tries hard but that the material in his weaker subjects is just too much for him at this time.

PERSONALITY AND SOCIAL ADJUSTMENT

Don is a quiet boy who rarely shows his feelings. His mother said that he rarely gets mad but when he does he really tears into "them";

she indicated she meant his brothers and/or sister. Don said that the only thing that really gets him mad is when people hit him and that he usually hits them back. "At home my bigger brother sometimes picks on me and I get so mad that I run out of the house and hide." When asked what causes his brother to get mad, he could give no reason but said, "He just gets mad at me."

Don seems to have few close friends and the number he actually plays with is even further reduced due to the fact that he is not within walking distance of anyone his age. At home he either plays with his younger brother or goes off by himself. Some of his solitary time is spent fishing in the summertime and trapping muskrats in the winter. He loves the outdoors.

Although he is usually shy and quiet, he does at times get very excited. This is especially noticeable when he believes that he is going to win a game he is playing. At these times he rubs his hands together and generally behaves in a nervous manner. For the most part, however, Don usually behaves as though nothing bothers him and that he can take a lot before he does anything about something that bothers him.

He gets along with his peers at school, but for the most part he spends his time with one or two boys. He rarely, if ever, speaks out in class and never asks for help on an assignment.

FAMILY HISTORY

Father

Mr. G. is a 46-year-old house painter who just recently changed employers because his former employer went bankrupt. At present he is idle because of a slack in the industry this time of year. He has an eighth-grade education and as such has been working at various jobs since his early teens. He was born and raised in the Midwest and has been married to Mrs. G. for 24 years.

He is a very quiet, unassuming person who seems quite content to take life on a day-to-day basis. There was no change in his
emotional behavior, whether he was talking about the weather, his
job, or his son's current difficulty. He was cooperative but never
volunteered any information during the interview. He talked only
when asked a direct question or when his wife looked at him for
confirmation of her verbalizations. At times, viewing his physical
presence was the only way to know he was still there.

Mother

Mrs. G. is 42 years old and spends her time as a housewife and
mother. She is much more assertive than her husband and seems to
be the driving force of the family. This was readily apparent during
the interview, as it was Mrs. G. who did most of the talking. She
did not seem to be overbearing but one got the idea that she took
the initiative because her husband was so unassertive, as well as it
being an inherent part of her everyday functioning. Her dominance
in the family unit was also apparent at the times when they both
came with Don during his testing sessions. It was Mrs. G. who drove
the car and on one occasion even waited in the car while her husband brought Don into the center. On only one occasion did Mr.
G. drive, and that was when he and Don came in alone.

Brothers and Sister

Jim, at 17 years of age, is the oldest and a sophomore in high school.
He was held back twice (Mrs. G.'s best recollection was the third
and sixth grades) because he could not do the work expected of
him. He was referred to the Child Guidance Center for a psychological evaluation. According to Mrs. G., they told her he was "too
young" for his age and recommended holding him back in school.
He is not having any difficulties at this time.

Not much was said about Lisa, 13 years old, except that she is not having any problems with school and seems to get along okay with Don. Don rarely mentioned her and, as is typical of a boy his age, said that he likes boys better than girls anyway.

Danny, 7 years old, is the one Don plays with the most. Mrs. G. said that they do get into squabbles but for the most part get along all right. Don indicated that he didn't mind sharing a room with his younger brother. Like Lisa, Danny seems to be functioning adequately in school at this time.

IMPRESSIONS

Mr. and Mrs. G. are rather content with their lives and have had children because church doctrine says that this is the right thing to do, to keep the house full of children, which necessarily cuts down on the one-to-one interactions, and possibly because of their own personal desire to have children. They are slow-moving people who rarely act out impulsively.

In many ways Don is very much like his father. Mr. G. is a pleasant man but rarely displays his feelings in an overt manner. Don is much the same way. Mr. G. only went as far as the eighth grade while his wife graduated from high school. Don is now in the fifth grade and is exhibiting some difficulty in some areas. Both Mr. G. and Don like the out-of-doors and Don is currently using the traps, for trapping muskrats, that his father used as a child.

Mr. and Mrs. G. are aware of much that goes on in family interaction but are not sure how to handle many situations. They are unaware of the developmental needs of their children. However, when it does come down to doing something about a recognized problem area, it is Mrs. G. who takes charge. She is the one who was not satisfied with one eye doctor's opinion and took Don to Dr. F.'s office. When it comes to taking care of the children, it is Mrs. G. who is the dominant parent.

The G.'s do care for Don and seem to be willing to help him in any way they can. Just now, however, they are unaware of the fact that it is the home situation that is a main contribution to Don's current mode of functioning. It may be difficult for them to accept this and more difficult to do something about it.

DISCUSSION OF THE INTAKE INTERVIEW

Within this intake interview there are seven major areas covered:

1. Problem (referring)
2. Informants
3. Home environment
4. Development
5. School environment
6. Personality and social adjustment
7. Family history
   Father
   Mother
   Siblings

The one final area, impressions, contains the interviewer's impressions and assessments of the family. The areas explored within this intake are broad, in an attempt to deal with the whole range of a child's functioning. However, within each area there are important missing pieces that would help us to understand this family more fully.

Problem

It would have been helpful had the interviewer explored the parent's understanding of Don's inability to "interpret what he sees," what they understand "psychometric testing" to mean, and what they expected from the total process. Also, why did they switch doctors if the first was of some help?

Informants

A fuller description of the process of the interview would have given the reader a clearer picture of parental interaction as well as the responsiveness of this couple to the interviewer's interventions. There is no assessment of the feeling tones or their evaluation over the course of the interview.

Home Environment

It is not clear whether or not Don was a participant in this intake interview. It would have been helpful to know from whom the information was obtained and when. It seems that some of the material comes from the parents while other data were reported by Don.

Development

This is the sketchiest section of the report, with most of the important data missing. There needs to be considerable exploration of the cesarean section: How did the mother feel about it? What was Don like at birth? How did she feel about him?

While Don may have had no major problems in being weaned, it does sound as if there were some problems. What were they? How was weaning accomplished? How was toilet training effected? At what ages did he sit up, crawl, stand, walk? How old was he when he first began to talk? What were his words? When did he begin to talk in sentences?

Other areas of development that needed exploration include Don's responses to each of the members of the family, the birth of his younger brother, and entrance into school. What was he like during the earlier years? Easy to handle? Hard to handle? Inquisitive?

School Environment

In this section it is clear that the interviewer visited the school Don attends but the motivations behind the visit have not been delineated. Furthermore, the child's full academic history has not been explored. One would also wish to know whether the interviewer observed in the classrooms as well as how Don responded to the visit.

Personality and Social Adjustment

Here there is a description of Don at present. As therapists, we would also be interested in whether this mode of functioning has been consistent over the years of the child's life or had there been a change at some point.

The specifics of Don's interactions with his siblings as well as with his parents are of crucial importance as it might clarify the nature of the relationship a therapist might expect. As Don plays games with his brother, it would be of interest to note the kinds of games he is interested in playing.

The parents, according to the report, do not seem to have much interaction with Don. Is this really the case? How do the parents handle the situation when Don gets mad? What makes him angry?

Family History

The descriptions of both parents are good as far as they go, but the parents are not embedded in their own families of origin. It would have been helpful to have data about the parents' families. Are these families part of the current functioning of Don's family?

The nature of the current marital situation is presented to us sketchily. The marriage has endured for 24 years, the oldest child is 17. How come there was a seven-year wait, especially if the family is Catholic? What was going on in the relationship?

Brothers and Sister

The other children are described sketchily and in terms of no apparent problems. One wonders whether this is actually what the parents said about them or this is the interviewer's distillation. In either case, a fuller personality sketch of the other children is necessary along with a more complete account of the troubles the older brother experienced that led to the referral to the child guidance clinic.

Impressions

Patently missing from this section are the impressions of the designated problem child and the developmental difficulties the child and his family are experiencing. At this point, it is not clear why the parents have come to the center other than that they were referred by the ophthalmologist.

The interviewer saw the child in his interaction with parents and obtained a beginning picture of the functioning of the child within the family; however, the problem as defined in this family is still the problem as parents have outlined it rather than as this child experienced it.

Children can neither fight against parental perceptions adequately, nor put into words the difficulties they are experiencing. A complete diagnostic assessment is therefore an indispensable part of the evaluation of children to determine problems and difficulties in living as experienced by the children, themselves, and not through someone else's eyes.

Appendix B:
Diagnostic Assessment

The psychological assessment of the child should include the following areas: intellectual, academic, perceptual, conceptual, and emotional functioning. The traditional battery of tests used are an individual intelligence test (Wechsler Intelligence Scale for Children [WISC-R], Stanford-Binet, Leiter, etc.), achievement and/or reading test, Bender-Gestalt, Rorschach, figure drawings, and thematic tests (e.g., Children's Apperception Test [CAT], Thematic Apperception Test [TAT], Michigan Picture Test [MPT]). A diagnostic play session could also be included (this functions as a trial run in therapy). This battery of tests yields a wealth of information from the child's perspective.

Now that we have tested the child, we must do something with our data. Below are a series of areas we need to consider, as well as the questions we must ask to gain the greatest possible understanding of the child.

To interpret the protocol accurately, each examiner must learn his own characteristics as a tester. Does he present himself as a teacher asking for the right answers? A permissive grandfather? An admired expert? A nonchalant parent? A threatening principal? One cannot carve out a neutral role in testing. Therefore, we must learn how children tend to view us, and then use this information in interpreting the results.

Child variables:

1. Hesitant responses
    Reserve
    Apprehension
    Self-protection
2. Active responses
    Friendliness
    Initiative
    Confidence
    Energy
    Speed
3. Obedience
4. Situational assessment
5. Thoughtfulness
6. Persistence
7. Acknowledgment of limitations
    Reaction to success
    Reaction to failure
8. Availability of appropriate experience
    Intellectuality
    Use of personal experience
    Openness to experience
    Fantasy

The above variables become incorporated into the report along with
a description of how the child looked as well as behavioral manifestations during the interview and testing proper.

Analysis of the test data proper could begin with the intellectual assessment. Questions that need be answered include:

1. What kind of thinker is this child?
    Can the child solve problems or only give factual answers,
    or can it use a combination of the two?

How does the child use the abstract and concrete modes of thinking?

2. What are the child's visual–motor abilities?
   What are the strengths and weaknesses?
   How does the child approach this kind of task?

3. What is the nature of the child's social comprehension?
   Does he know what is appropriate?
   Can he use this information, and how does he put it into effect?

4. Does the child have basic knowledge about his world?
   Does he have the basic facts?
   Where are the disabilities in the skills area or in problem solving?

5. How is the child's attention? Concentration?

6. Is the child more fluent with verbal skills or does he need to handle material to function adequately?
   Why do you think this is so?

7. Does the child function better in relationship with others or does he work better alone? Why?

8. On what kinds of tasks does he give up on?
   On what kinds of tasks does he persevere?

9. When does anxiety interfere with adequate functioning?
   How does this exhibit itself? Why?

As far as achievement testing is concerned, you are interested in how the results compare with intellectual achievement: What are the areas of strength and weakness? How did the child's response to the testing effect his or her achievement level? On the basis of both testings (intellectual and achievement), what can one expect of the child in an academic setting?

The child has strengths and weaknesses. Within this framework basic questions need to be addressed:

1. How does the child view his world?
    Does he see things in a vague, amorphous, undifferentiated manner?
    Does he approach things in a practical, down-to-earth fashion?
    Does he approach things in an integrated manner?
2. What is the child's general style of functioning and coping?
    How is this related to the way in which he views his world? Himself? His parents? His peers? His siblings?
3. How is the child's self-concept? Has the child made the appropriate identification? What is his conception of his role?
4. What are the conflict areas? What sets off the characteristic responses of his conflicts? How does the child handle the conflicts?
5. What is the nature of the child's impulse controls? His reality testing? His ego strength? Can he integrate his feelings? How does he handle anxiety?
6. What defenses does the child use and how are they employed?
7. Are there regressions or fixations and why?

A thorough knowledge of child development is indispensable in evaluating and understanding the underlying process of personality. All reports must be written in terms of what is appropriate for the age of the child. That is, are the findings appropriate for his developmental level? If not, why not?

Here is a sample report:

SAMPLE PSYCHOLOGICAL REPORT

Name: Sidney
Age: 13
Date of birth: 12/26/

Grade in school: 7
Parents: Sidney and Selma
Date of referral: 03/15/
Referred by: Dr. B.
Reason for referral: Sidney has been hospitalized with numer-
    ous physical complaints. Dr. B. asks for help in making
    differential diagnosis. What emotional problems may be
    contributing to somatic symptoms, including abdominal
    pain, back pain, headaches with nausea and dizziness, chest
    pain, and weakness with difficulty in walking. Is there
    evidence of organic brain damage?
Date of intake interview: 03/15, 03/16, 03/17, 03/19
Date of testing: 03/17, 03/18
Tests administered: House-Tree-Person-Figure Drawings
                     Bender-Gestalt Visual Motor Test
                     Wechsler Intelligence Scale for Children
                     Rorschach
                     Thematic Apperception Test

Description

Sidney is a handsome 13-year-old boy with even features, wide-set
gray-blue eyes with thick lashes, and shaggy dark blond hair. He is
rather thin, average in height, and dressed in hospital pajamas, robe,
and slippers. When Sidney was brought to the clinic office, in a
wheelchair, for testing, his face was strained and tense with apprehension showing slight flush of his pale complexion. Sidney seemed
wary; his eyes looked frightened, and he appeared to be wavering
between a shaky pose of adolescent nonchalance and a small boy's
tears. His manner vacillated from demanding petulance, to sarcasm
and irritation, to a disarming, appealing friendliness. There were brief
glimpses of his engaging grin, but Sidney never seemed free of an
underlying, threatening anxiety, even while he stubbornly insisted
that he had "no problems."

Background

Sidney is the sixth child in a family of eight children ranging in age from 28 to the unruly 8-year-old twin brothers. His 47-year-old mother, Selma, who is asthmatic, works as a nurse's aide, and was outspokenly resentful and bitter toward her husband, Sidney. She appears to be overprotective of her son, but also somewhat detached or uninvolved with his needs, preoccupied with marital conflict and the problems of her 14-year-old daughter, Anne. Anne, with her physical problems requiring multiple surgery, and her rape experience at school a year ago with resulting emotional disturbance and suicidal gesture, has been a continuing, dominant concern in the family. Sidney's father, 55 years old, is a bit awkward, and troubled with arthritis. He has an eighth grade education and works as a grounds supervisor. He seems inept, reluctant to deal with his son's problems, and like his wife, prefers to talk about Anne. He is vehement in his declaration that "the boy" should have been punished, and he appeared to be frustrated and feel helplessly ineffective in dealing with the family difficulties.

As a baby, Sidney was "easy to care for"; he "walked early and fed himself early." His mother remembers that he was "completely trained" when he was 15 months and "never wet the bed." She said that Sidney got "lots of loving" from his older sisters, and he always liked to "please people" and "loves attention." Selma's pregnancy with Sidney was unplanned, and she relates that her husband at first refused to believe that the baby was his child. She says that her husband always "blamed" Sidney for "pushing him off the farm," as this sixth child required him to earn more money to meet the financial needs of his family. (Selma also went to work when Sidney was 3½ years old.) In addition, the father has openly favored the twin boys, punishing Sidney when they deliberately "get him into trouble." In an unusual outburst of anger during a recent family skirmish, Sidney "hit his father back" and Selma told him it was wrong to strike his father. It seems evident that Sidney learned to please others, and avoid disapproval, by being a compliant, passive child with few problems, making few demands of his busy mother or his inadequate father.

Since the beginning of the current school year, Sidney has become increasingly restless, "nervous," and even "frantic" at times. He became very upset when he was required to shower with other boys in his gym class, saying he is "not right down there" (a reference to previous surgical correction of an undescended testicle), and has avoided school with various excuses. His mother's suggestions to shower earlier or later than the others would seem to confirm his belief in his sexual abnormality. Sidney's teachers comment that his attendance has been poor, that he is inattentive in class, and that his grades have dropped noticeably. He does not seem to have close friends, and appears to invite teasing by other children. Sidney has been considered a "pest" with his frequent, vague complaints regarding discipline, "fairness," and petty problems. Throughout the present school year, Sidney has continued to complain of varied physical disturbances, culminating in hospitalization in mid-January, and again in mid-March.

Behavior Observation

During testing procedures, Sidney complained repeatedly that he felt "rotten," that is, "my side is killing me," or "my head hurts, I can't think," and "I feel like I'm going to pass out." While his reactions seemed obviously exaggerated, as he grimaced or clutched his abdomen, the reality of his distress was apparent and seemed intensified following derogatory self-evaluation of his work, with self-deprecating remarks. However he continued to claim that he didn't worry because "my mom told me not to worry." He also resisted seeing a clinician since he had "no problems," but contradicted himself with a naive eagerness to talk about the brothers who "bug" him, and the gym class that he "despises." Sidney's responses, both in conversation and in testing, are often evasive, contradictory, and lacking in conviction betraying his need to "please others" and his utter lack of self confidence.

Test Results

Sidney is a bright adolescent boy, who feels extremely insecure, and who is experiencing a high level of anxiety, verging on panic as he struggles to control rising emotional impulses of aggressive and sexual nature. Threatening awareness of these feelings results in his intense anxiety, which is expressed in multiple somatic symptoms including abdominal pain, backaches, headaches, with nausea and dizziness, generalized body discomfort, and weakness with difficulty in walking. In desperate need of attention and help, Sidney's symptoms allow him to make use of the family's established pattern of reliance on physiological problem to gain a measure of concern and recognition for deep-seated emotional needs.

In spite of his high level of anxiety and physical complaints, Sidney achieved a Verbal Scale I.Q. of 113, a Performance Scale I.Q. of 107, and a Full Scale I.Q. of 111 on the Wechsler Intelligence Scale for Children. This places Sidney in the bright-normal range of intellectual functioning, at the 77th percentile in the population on which this test was standardized. While his overall verbal abilities are well above average, Sidney's initial, heightened uneasiness, stirring feelings of inadequacy and self-doubt, seemed to hamper his recall and use of school-related information. When uncertain about his competence, or the appropriateness of his response, Sidney tends to use annoying delay or avoidance tactics, such as asking, "Repeat the question." His nervous, flustered mannerisms lessened with recognition and appreciation of his successful efforts, and Sidney demonstrated a superior grasp of the significance of social issues with a strong ability to make sound judgments in practical, everyday situations. In addition, he has above-average understanding of complex ideas, relative to other children of his age. Sidney's language development as measured (in this test) by his understanding of word meanings is slightly below average, and is his weakest verbal skill. This may be, in part, a reflection of his family's rural, small-town culture, where there is apt to be less expectation and appreciation of highly developed literate skills.

Sidney's numerical skills and his abilities for memory and concentration are above average, as is his ability to recognize the essential details of his world. However, Sidney's problem solving falters when he is required to make evaluations of social situations, involving careful attention to the subtle nuances of interpersonal behavior in order to foresee consequences of these behaviors. Here, he works slowly, and finds it difficult to commit himself to a decision. When there are the implications of conflict, particularly with an authoritative, mothering woman, Sidney has trouble. He becomes uncertain, confused, and is inhibited by feelings of inadequacy and anxiety suggestive of underlying hostility. He has not developed age-appropriate self-reliance.

An important asset is Sidney's excellent ability for problem solving that requires manipulation of objects, with observation and analysis of spatial relationships. Sidney works with obvious satisfaction, in a systematic, evenly paced manner, effectively planning ahead without resorting to trial-and-error methods. His visual motor coordination is much above average and there is no indication of organic brain damage.

It is possible that Sidney's overall scores were somewhat lowered by generalized, subtle slowing of his thinking processes and responses. In several instances, he successfully solved problems in the overtime period. In subtests requiring manual dexterity, he achieved his high scores, largely without benefit of time bonuses. This may be an effect attributable to the central nervous system (CNS) depressant medications that Sidney was receiving.

Although Sidney is a bright boy, he has little confidence in his ability, and greatly needs confirmation of his achievements. In view of the intellectual strengths that Sidney demonstrates, it is likely that his abilities are not being fully utilized at present. Medication may be temporarily depressing his achievement in general, but more significantly the effect of Sidney's feelings of inadequacy, with his intense anxiety, contribute to indecisiveness, and self-doubting interferes with his intellectual functioning.

Sidney experiences pervasive feelings of insecurity and inferiority; he feels small, isolated, and helplessly inadequate to deal with his world. He views himself as excluded from his large family—the rejected child, resented by his father who blatantly favors his younger brothers. He thinks of himself as "stupid," "the troublemaker." Sidney is aware that somehow his mother holds him trapped in childhood, and he expects and feels that he deserves punishment for his wishes and attempts to become self-assertive, to "grow up." In addition, Sidney feels as if he "has a lot of work to do," he needs to become more competent, but he experiences his parents as unavailable to him. He must turn to others for help.

Sidney's extreme anxiety results from failure of his established ways of pushing from awareness, the disturbing impulses of aggression and hostility. As a young child he learned to maintain his mother's approval and affection, and to avoid his father's anger and punishments, by being the passive, undemanding, "good" child. His busy, distracted mother did not encourage or allow his early strivings for assertion, influencing him to remain compliant and cared for, to avoid her disapproval. As he also receives the subtle or overt messages of her resentment and hostility toward his father, Sidney fears her rejection of him since he is also male and carries his father's name. This contributes to his insecurity and anxiety.

At the same time Sidney experiences his father's rejection and is scapegoated as the child responsible for his father's disappointments and failures to attain his needs; Sidney cannot risk assertive behavior for fear of his father's punitive anger. Since his father not only rejects him but is himself an inept, inadequate model of masculinity, Sidney is further hampered in his growth toward maturity. In his untenable position, rejected and thwarted in his growth toward male competency, Sidney is experiencing extreme insecurity and inadequacy with accompanying hostility toward the parents that he must rely on. He also comes to feel that he is rejected because of his inadequacy, compounding his sense of helplessness and futility.

As Sidney reaches puberty, and is unable to suppress his natural sexual feelings, he is caught in a panic. Since male sexuality holds fear of further rejection from his mother, he is pulled to remain little and cared for, as is natural but overimportant in his experience, at the same time that he is pulled to somehow deny his masculinity. In addition, maleness carries a further ominous threat to Sidney since his own sexual urges are not well understood and may well have frightening implications for him because of his sister's rape experience. This, with his father's strongly punitive attitude and threat of severe retribution to the boy involved, builds Sidney's fears and increases guilt feelings, which are present naturally in a small boy's sexual development in relationship to his mother and father. He is caught in conflict, between allowing natural male impulses, and the opposite compliant, more feminine attitudes that deny masculinity. Sidney cannot move to gain satisfaction of his great affectional needs in his customary way, in closeness to his mother, or sisters, for fear of the erotic feelings that threaten to intrude into his awareness.

In addition, Sidney's predicament is accentuated at school in relation to others his age, where he is being rejected as an inadequate and incompetent peer. He can be expected to suffer ridicule from boys his age for any display of weak, "feminine" characteristics, and cannot risk expression of his hostility here as well, for fear of further rejection. He would be particularly vulnerable to taunts of "homo" from boys in gym, since he is already convinced of his sexual abnormality of being "not right down there."

Since Sidney has experienced overt rejection by his father in favor of his twin brothers, he has strong feelings of hostility toward them as well as his father. This is easily aroused when the younger boys irritate him with invasion of his privacy and innumerable annoyances. When Sidney's retaliation gets him into trouble, he is trapped in an impossible position where the upsurge of frustration and hostility becomes unmanageable. He acts in impulsive physical outbursts, or more indirect exasperating, defiant mannerisms, bringing compounded parental anger and punishment. While Sidney's mother sends him messages of understanding, and being on his side, she does not actively help him. She contributes further to his desperate position by adding to his guilt, admonishing him that he should not hit his father.

Sidney has felt excluded from his family; in order to have some measures of approval and acceptance, he has needed to be the child without problems. In this family, however, where the parents are inept, the father is distant, and the mother is overburdened and resentful, children have learned to make use of physical problems in order to command parental attention and action on their behalf. Here, too, Sidney is bound in conflict. It is not surprising that he must deny that he has problems, at the same time that he wildly exaggerates his complaints, and becomes evasive and contradictory as well.

There is a strong manipulative aspect of Sidney's exaggeration of his symptoms. His real physiological disturbances serve to remove him from threatening situations of stress at school and at home, as well as to gain attention and response to his great need for support and help. Sidney has learned to maximize this second use of "being sick" in ways that appear to be partially conscious and therefore add to his feelings of guilt, ways that also carry a subtle expression of his underlying hostility.

Summary

This highly intelligent boy, who cannot allow awareness of expression of his hostile feelings toward father, mother, or twin brothers, experiences strong feelings of guilt and intense anxiety that are largely expressed in overwhelming, variable somatic symptoms. This extreme anxiety is heightened by fears directly related to the sexual changes of puberty, which carry greater threat for Sidney than is usual for teenage boys and increases the natural sexual ambivalence. He is desperately needing attention and help, but must pretend to have no problems in order to maintain a semblance of self-respect and approval.

As his efforts to ward off and control threatening aggressive and sexual impulses fail, Sidney experiences greater intensity and guilt along with increased feelings of insecurity, inadequacy, and helplessness. This leads to desperate measures including exaggeration of physical discomfort to ensure that his needs of being cared for are met. Sidney's above-average level of intellectual functioning and perceptual motor acuity contraindicate the presence of organic brain damage.

Recommendations

1. Psychotherapy:
   a. Male therapist for the development of a relationship in which Sidney can affirm his masculinity through identification with a strong masculine model, and learn to be assertive in gaining for himself the things that he needs, that is, satisfaction of affectional needs, respect and approval from others, including needed privacy from twin brothers within his family, with increased competency leading to more self-confidence and self-esteem in keeping with his real abilities.
   b. The support of an effective adult advocate who will act as necessary for Sidney's best interests, with his direction, that is, possible excuse from gym until Sidney forms a more comfortable confidence in his sexual normalcy, and removal of threat of physical punishment (the gym teacher's use of wooden paddle), in consultations with parents, the school counselor, and Sidney's teachers.
   c. Legitimization of aggressive and hostile feelings, distinguishing the validity and acceptability of wishes and feel-

ings from unacceptable or destructive actions, to lessen
Sidney's heavy burden of guilt.

   d. Educational, honest information regarding facts and
implications of physiological findings, sexual changes at
puberty, and the results of psychological testing.

2. Family therapy or marital counseling with Sidney's parents
in conjunction with individual therapy for Sidney, to deal
with parental needs as individuals and to support and teach
more adequate parenting.

3. Optometrist or ophthalmologist's examination for evaluation of visual complaints, to determine if Sidney needs
glasses.

4. Discontinue drug therapy on trial basis if all the physicians
concur, as EEG abnormality may be of long-standing nature
and not responsible for Sidney's symptoms and complaints,
dependent on the results of neurological evaluation.

Informing Interview

The adolescent should be at the informing interview. A younger child
should have an informing interview by himself with the therapist.

    Parents know most of the information that is collected during
the course of the psychological examination: holding back data
because it might be unpalatable is not helpful. The therapist must
tell the truth at all times with great tact. However, truth is not an
absolute; it is relative to the situation, the time, and the people we
work with. Therefore, truth is a process. We share what we can of
the truth, for our own comfort and what our clients are able to hear.
Within these limitations, we share our findings from psychological
testing. Furthermore, as therapists we are committed to growth and
change, which means that our findings are not firmly entrenched,
unchangeable facts. Our findings are a sample of behavior at a specific time and under specific circumstances of the person's life situation. As changes occur, so will the findings of our psychological

examination. The assessment tells us how the child views his life situation from his own perspective and not from the perspective of parents. We develop a treatment plan and modality to focus our work more accurately, and from there, as the person changes and grows, we alter our methodology and reassess the individual on an ongoing basis. However, children cannot put their feelings, knowledge, and understandings into words. This limitation at the beginning of the therapeutic work necessitates the assessment to help us to avoid the pitfalls and blind alleys that are so inherent in work with children without an adequate assessment.

The major problems child therapists have with their clients is their identification with their young clients and the viewing of the parents as enemies. We must keep in mind that without the parents the child would not have been brought to see us, so that even the most "horrible" of parents do have real concerns about their children, and it is this concern that will enable us to help the child most fully.

The informing interview establishes the treatment plan, for along with a sharing of the findings, we make recommendations. Encouraging parents to enter their own therapy may be an ideal; it is not always reached and we therefore must compromise with the reality of finances or the psychological makeup of the parents. What we do work with are the basic concerns of the parents for their child, what is happening to their child, and what the therapist is doing with their child. While viewing the therapy session of the child is an invasion of the child's privacy, periodic conferences with the parents, not only to share your understandings of the child but also to find out what is happening with the child outside of the therapeutic process, are crucial.

References

Axline, V. (1947). *Play Therapy*. New York: Houghton Mifflin.

Beaudet, D. (1990). *Encountering the Monster*. New York: Continuum.

Benedek, E. P. (1984). *The Secret Worry*. New York: Human Sciences Press.

Berlin, I. N. (1987). Some transference and countertransference issues in the playroom. *Journal of the American Academy of Child and Adolescent Psychiatry* 26(1):101–107.

Bornstein, B. (1948). Emotional barriers in the understanding and treatment of young children. *American Journal of Orthopsychiatry* 18:691–697.

Bretherton, I. (1984). *Symbolic Play: The Development of Social Understanding*. Orlando, FL: Academic Press.

Brooks, R. (1985). The beginning sessions of child therapy: of messages and metaphors. *Psychotherapy* 22(4):761–769.

Caplan, P. J., and Hall-McCorquodale, I. (1985). Mother-blaming in major clinical journals. *American Journal of Orthopsychiatry* 55(3): 345–353.

Consumer Reports (1995). Does therapy help? *Consumer Reports* 60(11): 734–739.

Ekstein, R. (1966). *Children of Time and Space of Action and Impulse*. New York: Appleton-Century-Crofts.

——— (1981). Some thoughts concerning the clinical use of children's dreams. *Bulletin of the Menninger Clinic* 45(2):115–124.

Erikson, E. (1950). *Childhood and Society*. New York: Norton.

Fenichel, O. (1945). *The Psychoanalytic Theory of Neurosis*. New York: Norton.

Flapan, D., and Neubauer, P. (1972). Developmental groupings of preschool children. *Israel Annals of Psychiatry and Related Disciplines* 10(1): 52–90.

Foulkes, D. (1982). *Children's Dreams: Longitudinal Studies*. New York: Wiley.

——— (1990). Dreaming and consciousness. *European Journal of Cognitive Psychology* 2(1):39–55.

Freud, A. (1965a). *The Psychoanalytical Treatment of Children.* New York: International Universities Press.

——— (1965b). The relations between child analysis and adult analysis. In *Normality and Pathology in Childhood: Assessment of Development,* pp. 25–81. New York: International Universities Press.

——— (1970). Problems of termination in child analysis. *Writings* 7:3–21.

Freud, S. (1900). The interpretation of dreams. *Standard Edition* 4/5:1–626.

——— (1905). Three essays on the theory of sexuality. *Standard Edition* 7:125–145.

Friend, M. (1972). Psychoanalysis of adolescents. In *Handbook of Child Psychoanalysis,* ed. B. B. Wolman. New York: Van Nostrand Reinhold.

Furman, E. (1982). Mothers have to be there to be left. *Psychoanalytic Study of the Child* 37:15–28. New Haven: Yale University Press.

Ginott, H. (1968). Interpretations and child therapy. *Voices* 4:40–43.

Kaplan, L. (1978). *Oneness and Separateness: From Infant to Individual.* New York: Touchstone.

Kennedy, H. (1977). The role of insight in child analysis: a developmental viewpoint. *Journal of the American Psychoanalytic Association* 27:9–28.

Kernberg, O. (1975). *Borderline Conditions and Pathological Narcissism.* New York: Jason Aronson.

Klein, M. (1975). *The Psychoanalysis of Children,* trans. A. Strachey. New York: Delta.

LaClave, L. J., and Brack, G. (1989). Reframing to deal with patient resistance: practical application. *American Journal of Psychotherapy* 43(1):68–76.

Lewis, M. (1972). Interpretation in child analysis. *American Association of Child Psychiatry* 11:32–53.

Lichtenberg, J. (1983). *Psychoanalysis and Infant Research.* Hillsdale, NJ: Analytic Press.

Lovinger, S. L. (1974). Socio-dramatic play and language development in preschool disadvantaged children. *Psychology in the Schools* 11(3): 313–320.

Lynn, D. B. (1974). *The Father: His Role in Child Development.* Monterey, CA: Brooks/Cole.

Mack, J. (1965). Nightmares, conflict and ego development in childhood. *International Journal of Psycho-Analysis* 46:404–428.

Mahler, M. (1968). *On Human Symbiosis and the Vicissitudes of Individuation, Vol. I: Infantile Psychosis.* New York: International Universities Press.

Marshall, R. J. (1979). Countertransference in the psychotherapy of children and adolescents. *Contemporary Psychoanalysis* 15(4):595–629.

——— (1982). *Resistant Interactions.* New York: Human Sciences Press.

Mayle, P. (1973). *Where Did I Come From?* Secaucus, NJ: Lyle Stuart.

McClelland, D., Atkinson, J., Clark, R., and Lowell, E. (1953). *The Achievement Motive.* New York: Appleton.

Norman, J. (1989). The analyst's visual images and the child analyst's trap. *Psychoanalytic Study of the Child* 44:117–135. New Haven, CT: Yale University Press.

Novick, J. (1982). Termination: themes and issues. *Psychoanalytic Quarterly* 2:29–365.

——— (1990). Comments on termination in child, adolescent and adult analysis. *Psychoanalytic Study of the Child* 45:419–436. New Haven, CT: Yale University Press.

Opie, I., and Opie, P. (1950/1980). *The Lore and Language of Schoolchildren.* London: Oxford University Press.

——— (1969). *Children's Games in Street and Playground.* Oxford: Oxford University Press.

——— (1992). *I Saw Esau.* Cambridge, MA: Candlewick.

Ornstein, A. (1976). Making contact with the inner world of the child. *Comprehensive Psychiatry* 17(1):3–36.

Parke, R. D. (1981). *Fathers.* Cambridge, MA: Harvard University Press.

Piaget, J. (1952). *The Origins of Intelligence in Chiildren,* trans. M. Cook. New York: International Universities Press.

Redl, F., and Wineman, D. (1957). *The Aggressive Child.* Glencoe, IL: Free Press.

Reich, A. (1960/1973). Further remarks on counter-transference. In *Annie Reich: Psychoanalytic Contributions,* pp. 271–287. New York: International Universities Press.

Rubenstein, A., Zager, K., and Gottsegen, G. (1991). *Psychotherapy with Children and Adolescents: A Guide for Parents.* Brochure. Phoenix, AZ: American Psychological Association, Div. of Psychotherapy.

Sandler, J., Kennedy, H., and Tyson, R. L. (1975). Discussions on transference. *Psychoanalytic Study of the Child* 30:409–442. New Haven,
CT: Yale University Press.

Sarnoff, C. (1976). *Latency.* New York: Jason Aronson.

Shirk, S. R., ed. (1988). *Cognitive Development and Child Psychotherapy.*
New York: Plenum.

Singer, J. L. (1973). *The World of Make-Believe.* New York: Academic Press.

Smilansky, S. (1968). *The Effects of Socio-Dramatic Play on Disadvantaged
Pre-School Children.* New York: Wiley.

Spiegel, S. (1989). *An Interpersonal Approach to Child Therapy.* New York:
Columbia University Press.

Stern, D. (1973). *The Interpersonal World of the Infant.* New York: Basic Books.

Stolorow, R. D., and Lachmann, F. M. (1980). *Psychoanalysis of Developmental Arrests.* New York: International Universities Press.

Sullivan, H. S. (1953). *The Interpersonal Theory of Psychiatry.* New York:
Norton.

Thorne, B. (1993). *Gender Play.* New Brunswick, NJ: Rutgers University Press.

Tolpin, M. (1971). On the beginning of a cohesive self: an application
of the concept of transmuting internalizations to the study of the
transitional object and signal anxiety. *Psychoanalytic Study of the Child*
26:316–352. New Haven, CT: Yale University Press.

Tompkins, S. (1963). *Affect, Imagery, and Consciousness,* vols. 1 and 2. New
York: Springer.

Van Dam, H. (1967). Relatos de mesas redondas de las associacion psico-
analiticas Americana: problemas transfericiales en el anatisis de ninos.
[Roundtable reports of the American Psychoanalytic Association:
Transferential problems in the analysis of children.] *Revista de Psico-
analisis* 24(4):925–935.

Waksman, J. D. (1986). The countertransference of the child analyst.
International Review of Psycho-Analysis 13:405–415.

White, R. W. (1959). *Ego and Reality in Psychoanalytic Theory.* New York:
International Universities Press.

Winnicott, D. W. (1958/1965). The capacity to be alone. In *The Maturational Process and the Facilitating Environment.* Madison, CT: International Universities Press.

———— (1977). *The Piggle.* New York: International Universities Press.

Index